Sappho in Love

A Comedy in Two Acts

By Carolyn Gage

What critics are saying ...

"Gage's script romps along with sexy smarts and lubricious hilarity... filled with memorable lines and saucy double-entendres."—*The Isthmus,* Madison, WI.

"... hardly a minute goes by that the theater does not fill up with laughter... entertaining and wildly pleasing to the audience."—*The Badger Herald* (Univ. of Wisconsin-Madison), Madison, WI.

"... deliciously comic, off-kilter... a charming, affectionate portrait of young women coming to terms with their longings—for both independence and romantic fulfillment."—*Chicago Reader.*

"... *Sappho in Love* disproves the old canard about lesbians lacking a sense of humor... These are some funny, funny lesbians."—*Sacramento News and Reviews.*

"delicious... sweet, funny, moving, tender... eminently playable... richly imagined, perfectly conceived piece..."—John Stoltenberg, author and activist.

What audiences are saying (from the Sacramento website www.seeaplay.com):

"I caught this show last night at their sold out opening and laughed until my sides hurt. Seriously, the whole audience was howling. If you're in the mood for a great comedy on a weekend night to help beat the heat, this is the one to see. By which I mean I expect this show to sell out fast if last night's audience has any say in the matter... THE smash hit of the summer."

Sappho In Love was a fast moving, funny take on classical Greek comedies. I am not a lesbian, nor was the person I went with, yet we enjoyed it very much. I will probably take some other friends to see this..."

"... *Sappho in Love* was not what I expected it to be. It was a fun, sassy show that had the audience laughing throughout."

"My partner and I were looking for a romantic date night activity and happened upon this phenomenal play! Touching, funny, gregarious—well worth the money! For anyone who enjoys the theater, *Sappho in Love* is one of the most side-splitting two hours you can have! Hysterical, sweet and just a little different! See the play and tell your friends!"

"I thought this play was so funny. I laughed the entire time. I am telling everyone not to miss it. Good job, Lambda. One of your best!"

"I watched *Sappho* on Friday the 18th and must have laughed every twenty seconds for two hours. This play is unique, well-produced, and you shouldn't miss it… The play is charming, energizing, and I'm so happy to have seen it!"

"You don't have to be a Lesbian to enjoy the machinations of the three goddesses of love as they plot and scheme to win control of Lesbos and eventually The World! This show is a total romp."

Sappho in Love is a riotous romp across the slippery terrain of Lesbian romance, as the goddesses on Olympus come down to earth to recruit among Sappho and her followers.

Artemis, the Goddess of Lesbian Celibacy, and Hera, the Goddess of Monogamy, join forces to challenge Aphrodite, the Goddess of Lust, for her hegemony on Lesbos. Sappho, the great poet and teacher on the island, is a devotee of Aphrodite, and because of this, her school has become a center for the cult of lesbian sexuality and romantic love. Artemis, denouncing Aphrodite's use of her intoxicating nectar to attract followers, vows to found a rival school on Lesbos where young girls will be weaned away from Sappho's decadent teachings to learn the more sober arts of wilderness survival.

But Artemis underestimates the power of lesbian seduction, when Aphrodite sends Persuasion, her handmaiden, to enroll in outdoor school—and when the Goddess of Celibacy finds herself entangled with the Slave of Desire, she discovers that freedom without intimacy can be as meaningless as intimacy without freedom.

Meanwhile... Sappho herself is experiencing girl trouble when her longsuffering partner, fed up with Sappho's infidelities, begins to date another woman. Add to the midsummer mix-up, the arrival of a new student who can't wait to taste the pleasures of Lesbian life, and the painful trials of a student whose best friend is on the eve of leaving the island to marry a soldier.

Sapphic poetry abounds amid meteor showers, midsummer eve trysts, masquerades and melodramas—all overseen by the benevolent trio of lesbian "*deae ex machina!*" Throw in a rowdy troupe of soaking-wet naiads and it all adds up to a tasty dish of lesbian comedy. In the end, the couples sort themselves out, for better or worse, and Hera pronounces her blessings on a new matriarchal order.

10 women, 1 little girl, unspecified number of chorus members
2 hours
Multiple sets

INTRODUCTION

Sappho in Love is a celebration of lesbian community with a mission of healing.

Lesbians have come into our sexual orientation as outlaws and defectors from hetero-patriarchal culture. As few of us were raised by lesbians in lesbian households, we have not had the privilege of growing up immersed in lesbian culture. We have had to piece together our lesbian identities, usually as adults, from leftover or remodeled aspects of former heterosexual identities, from the flotsam and jetsam of lesbian cultural artifacts floating in mainstream culture, from various enclaves of lesbian underground communities and political movements, or from the painstakingly recovered lesbian histories and literature of recent decades. Our relationships can reflect the dominant-submissive gender roles from patriarchy, or the "fusion" that occurs when two co-dependents lose themselves in each other, or the trauma and drama of the sexual compulsive.

I wanted to write about my beloved lesbian people, about the way we love— or try to love—each other, and I wanted to offer a playful, but serious analysis that held out a strong possibility of healing for all of us.

I use three archetypal goddesses from classical mythology to represent three modes of lesbian relationships: Hera, for stultifying domestic coupledom; Aphrodite, for obsessive-compulsive sexual liaisons; and Artemis, for "stone butch" celibacy. I put these goddesses in competition with each other for the heart of Sappho, the great poet and teacher of Lesbos. The stakes are raised when the slave of Aphrodite falls in love with the goddess of celibacy, and the irresistible force meets the immoveable object.

The subplots concern the young women, themselves—the Lesbians in Sappho's school: Will Atthis be able to persuade her best friend to cancel her wedding in favor of a lesbian love? Will Timas, the new arrival, succeed in her mission to come out as a lesbian? Will Sappho's longsuffering girlfriend find the strength to leave her unfaithful lover?

Heaven comes down to earth as the goddesses disguise themselves as humans to mix it up with mortals. The play becomes a kind of lesbian midsummer night's dream with poetry contests, meteor showers, lessons on lesbian love-making, romantic trysting, mix-ups and disguises.

This is a play with a large cast, and it was my intention that every member of my audience be able to see some aspect of herself and her relationships in the characters and situations on stage. I wanted to give us all a chance to laugh at ourselves, but also see ourselves with compassion. My community has been deeply polarized around relationship issues—and especially around sexual relationships. In *Sappho in Love*, we can see the stereotyping from all points of view and begin to envision the integration that, I believe, can bring personal healing as well as healing to our communities.

SAPPHO IN LOVE

CAST OF CHARACTERS

PERSUASION: A young woman, androgynous in appearance.

APHRODITE: An older woman, impersonating a drag queen.

ARTEMIS: An older butch with an impressive physique.

HERA: An older fem, very domestic.

SAPPHO: A butch womanizer in her early forties.

ATTHIS: A young, butch athlete.

GONGYLA: A fem woman in her late thirties or early forties.

GORGO: A butch in her late thirties or early forties.

ANACTORIA: A young woman.

TIMAS: A young woman, a geek.

YOUNG NAIAD: A young woman.

SAPPHO'S STUDENTS / NAIADS: No fewer than five young women.

SCENE

The temples of Aphrodite and Hera, and the grove of Artemis, all located on Lesbos.

TIME

Lesbian archetypal time.

Note on staging: *Sappho in Love* was originally written for outdoor production, with no set changes. Set changes disrupt the flow of scenes and slow the pacing, and it is recommended that indoor productions retain the simplicity of the original staging.

The translations of Sappho's poems are by the following poets:

"A Hymn to Venus," Ambrose Phillips, 1711.
Fragment 40, "On Soft Cushions," J. M. Edmonds, 1922.
Fragment 77, "Delight nor Pain," Michael Field,1889.
Fragment 32, "To Gongyla," J. M. Edmonds, 1922.
Fragment 116, "O Beauteous One," David Moore Robinson, 1925.
Fragment 117, "Can It Be," Henry T. Wharton, 1877
Fragment 46, "To the Graces," Edwin Marion Cox, 1924.
Fragment 110, "Wedding Song," J. M. Edmonds, 1922.
Frament 140, "Happy Bridegroom," Edwin Marion Cox, 1924.
Fragment 109, "To the Bride," H. DeVere Stackpole.
Fragment 121, "To Her Virginity," H. DeVere Stackpole.
Fragment 112, "Like the Apple," H. DeVere Stackpole.
Fragment 113, "Like the Hyacinth," Dante Gabriel Rossetti, 1870.
Fragment 5, "To Aphrodite," Henry T. Wharton, 1877.
Fragment 3, "Moonlight," H. DeVere Stackpole.
Frament 51, "No Revenge," J. M. Edmonds, 1922.
Fragment 92, "To A Rival, In Irony," J. M. Edmonds, 1922.
Fragment 82, "As Round an Altar," Michael Field, 1889.
Fragment 83, "The Cretan Women," H. DeVere Stackpole.
Fragment 74, "Come, Graces," H. DeVere Stackpole.
Fragment 63, "To Atthis," J.M. Edmonds, 1922.
Fragment 81, "The Moon Has Set," J. Addington Symonds, 1885.
Fragment 53, "Fame," J. M. Edmonds, 1922.

SAPPHO IN LOVE

ACT I

SCENE 1

Lights come up on Aphrodite's temple on Lesbos. The temple is on the edge of a cliff, and the view of the ocean is spectacular, as rosy-fingered dawn appears.

PERSUASION, a young slave woman, androgynous in the Mary-Martin sense, lies sleeping on a stone bench. She is dressed in a shimmering chiton. On the altar is a brass decanter. A voice is heard offstage—from overhead, if possible:

APHRODITE: *(Offstage.)* Persuasion! Oh, Persuasion! *(The young woman stirs in her sleep.)* Persuasion! Oh, Persuasion, my girl… Sweet and lovely Persuasion, where are you? *(The young woman turns restlessly in her sleep. APHRODITE calls sharply:)* Persuasion! Answer me!

PERSUASION: *(She wakes with a start and looks up toward the clouds.)* What? Here I am, mistress. Here I am… *(An aside.)* Where am I? *(Looking around.)* Let's see… That looks like Mt. Ida… *(Turning the other direction.)*… and there's Mt. Olympus… So, that would be the coast of Aeolis over there… Well, this can only mean one thing. *(Speaking to the voice.)* Mistress, it appears I'm at your temple on the isle of Lesbos.

APHRODITE: *(Offstage.)* Good, good! That's exactly where I need you. I'm expecting company this afternoon and I want you to help entertain them. How's the supply of nectar?

PERSUASION: *(Checking the decanter on the altar.)* Almost empty.

APHRODITE: *(Offstage.)* I'll bring some more. Be a good girl and set out the goblets. Three of them. I'll be down in a minute.

PERSUASION: Yes, mistress. *(Slumping again on the bench.)* Oh, was there ever a slave more miserable than I, Persuasion, handmaiden of Aphrodite! I know what you're thinking. You're thinking, "Gee, tough life being the slave to the Goddess of Love." Well, it's not all being on your knees, you know. *(She crosses behind the altar, retrieving a tray with three exotic goblets. One of the goblets is purple.)* No, it's my job to get women to fall in love with each other. Not exactly a walk in the park, if you know what I mean. The older women, for example. They see me coming, and they head for the hills.

1

The young women—they're easy, but, goddess, do they complain! First they'll die if she doesn't notice them. Then they'll die if she *does* notice them. Then they'll die if she leaves. And then, they'll die if she *doesn't* leave… It seems that no matter what I do for them, they're still dissatisfied. But it's not the work I mind so much. It's the ethics. I mean, let's face it, women in love are worthless. Well—aren't they? Staring out the window all day, kissing their pillows all night. There's only one woman I know who can work when she's in love, and that's Sappho—but she's a poet, so that doesn't count. No, women in love are hopeless. And it's all my fault. You see, I drug them. Yeah. With Aphrodite's nectar. I used to think it was fun, but that was before it happened to me. Yeah. That's right. I'm in love. Is that a joke, or what? Me, Persuasion, the one who makes everyone else fall in love and act like an idiot. Aphrodite would kill me if she knew. And you want to know what's worse? The woman I'm in love with is her arch-rival. You know who I'm talking about, don't you? Artemis, the Goddess of Celibacy. Is that perfect or what? Artemis strong, independent, self-reliant Artemis. Never had any lovers, never will have any. Doesn't need them, doesn't want them, doesn't even believe in love. The absolutely most unavailable person in the whole universe, and that's who the Slave of Love picks to crush out on. And you think you've got problems! Of course, Artemis hasn't even noticed me. How could she? I'm just a slave and she's a goddess, and besides she hates Aphrodite. So, that's that. Not much I can do about it, except in my dreams. That's what I was doing just now, before Aphrodite woke me up. I was dreaming I was in Arcadia with Artemis—that's where she lives. And I was her slave, and I was walking behind her, carrying her arrows for her. And she was walking in front of me, with those broad shoulders, and those muscular arms—and those *capable* hands. Goddess, those hands! Anyway, she's walking ahead of me, and I'm following behind, and then suddenly she turns around and asks me for an arrow, and I go to hand it to her, only her fingers brush against mine accidentally, and there's this spark between us, and her eyes meet mine, and the next thing I know, I'm in her arms… *(Closing her eyes and hugging herself.)*… and she's bending over me whispering to me in that husky voice of hers—

APHRODITE: *(A shrill voice from offstage.)* Persuasion! My little Persuasion! Where are you?

PERSUASION: *(Her eyes fly open.)* That's not her.

APHRODITE: *(Entering.)* Not who, dear? *(APHRODITE, an older woman, is dressed like an over-the-top drag queen. She carries a large decanter.)*

PERSUASION: Nothing, mistress. I was… asleep.

APHRODITE: And dreaming of my delights. I know, I understand. You needn't be ashamed, dear girl. You couldn't help yourself. Indeed, who can? For am I not Aphrodite, the great Goddess of Love herself?—the embodiment of all womanly desire, the personification of all female grace and allure, the very essence and quintessence of gynecoid tumescence.

PERSUASION: *(An aside.)* "Gynecoid?"

APHRODITE: Why, *I* even have dreams about myself! But this is no time for us to sit around and feminate! We must hurry, because our company will be here any minute, and I want us to be prepared when they arrive.

PERSUASION: Who are they?

APHRODITE: My rivals. No, not rivals—for the Goddess of Love has no parallel… Horizontal, yes—parallel, no. Let us say, "challengers." Yes, two challengers who envy the power your mistress wields over the hearts of mortal women.

PERSUASION: Who are these challengers?

APHRODITE: Hera, the Goddess of Marriage, and Artemis, the Goddess of Celibacy.

PERSUASION: Artemis!

APHRODITE: Yes, I know—it's really a joke, isn't it, to think that celibacy could hold a candle to sexual passion, but you know how Artemis is.

PERSUASION: *(Horrified.)* Artemis is coming here—today?

APHRODITE: This very hour. She and Hera have requested a summit meeting to decide once and for all which goddess shall control the destinies of women. As if women haven't already chosen for themselves. But, the Goddess of Marriage and the Goddess of Celibacy seem to feel that I exercise an unfair advantage, a common charge brought by the less popular goddesses. Well, I have nothing to hide, and if a meeting will make them feel better about their empty temples and barren altars, then a meeting we shall have. But here's what I want you to do, Persuasion: While I listen to our disgruntled guests, I want you to practice a little of your persuasive arts—
PERSUASION: *(Interrupting in a panic.)* But I have no power over Artemis! She is the only goddess who is immune to my spells.

APHRODITE: You didn't let me finish! *(An aside.)* Younger women never do. *(To PERSUASION.)* I want you to serve them my nectar.

PERSUASION: But—

APHRODITE: For there are none on Olympus—or on earth—who are immune to its intoxicating power. *(She takes her decanter and passes it under PERSUASION's nose.)* One part the first dew of the morning, gathered from the tender petals of the sweet and blushing violet—soft, tremulous petals, nestled in their little thickets like fragrant clusters of jewels—and a second part… *(Tracing a finger down PERSUASION's face and onto her breast.)*… the tears of a maiden for her first love—salty, bittersweet— melting on the tongue—oh, the sighs, the tempests and the torments of that first precocious love—the intoxicating effluvium of a young woman's first crush… *(Crossing down center.)* And finally the third and most potent ingredient of them all— my own sweet juice… *(She dips her fingers in the nectar and smells them.)*… the cyprian honey that flows from the sacred cleft in the temple of the Goddess of Love herself, Aphrodite, mistress of all passion, empress of all desire, supreme sultana—

PERSUASION: *(Interrupting.)* You want me to *drug* Artemis with your nectar?

APHRODITE: So harsh a word, my sweet. I want you to *persuade* her.

PERSUASION: But she'll never touch it! She calls it poison! Artemis has a horror of any kind of intoxication.

APHRODITE: And that is where I am counting on you to use a little artifice, my dear. You shall tell her it's spring water.

PERSUASION: You want me to lie?

APHRODITE: It's your best feature.

PERSUASION: But I can't lie to Artemis!

APHRODITE: And why not?

PERSUASION: Because she's… she's… she's—

APHRODITE: What?

PERSUASION: The Goddess of Integrity. *(There is a chilling silence.)*

APHRODITE: Funny—I almost detect a note of respect in your voice.

PERSUASION: Oh, no, Mistress. I only—

APHRODITE: You aren't contemplating a defection, are you?

PERSUASION: No, Mistress—

APHRODITE: It would almost sound as if you would like to trade your soft and silky chiton—which, by the way, is most becoming in that it promises more than it delivers—for the coarse and smelly bearskins with which your "Goddess of Integrity" covers her own sunburnt and questionably groomed hide—*(PERSUASION tries to speak, but she is cut off.)* It would almost sound as if you are weary of that palatial bower on Mt. Helicon, with its cloud of downy pillows from which you trace the nightly travels of the evening star in her graceful transit across the inky empyrean—that you would prefer instead to pass your nights on the cold and rocky heights of Arcadia's wildest haunts, in bruised and restless privation, sharing your frigid billet with our Lady of the Beasts—*(PERSUASION starts to speak again, but is cut off again.)* It would almost sound as if my lovely Persuasion has tired of ambrosia and nectar—mind you, the very honey nectar of her own most generous mistress—o ungrateful minion!—the very nectar for which the entire mortal world, like puppies brawling at a bitch's tit, will gouge and gore themselves to death—that this very nectar of the Goddess of Love has spoiled your palate and left you with an insatiable craving for the redoubtable blandishments of Arcadia—to wit: raw deer meat, tree fungus, and insect larvae.

PERSUASION: Mistress, I meant no offense.

APHRODITE: And none was taken. *(A hand on her shoulder.)* Now, you will serve the nectar to Artemis.

PERSUASION: What about Hera? Do I lie to her, too?

APHRODITE: Oh, no, that won't be necessary.

PERSUASION: Why not?

APHRODITE: Because the Goddess of Marriage is a nectar-holic. *(PERSUASION registers surprise.)* Don't tell me you didn't know? If it weren't for the intoxication of sex, she'd never get anyone to the altar. So— now, pay attention, dear. We'll pour nectar into these two goblets, for our guests. *(She pours from her decanter.)* There... And then water in this one, for me... *(She fills the purple goblet with water.)*

PERSUASION: You're not drinking nectar?

APHRODITE: Not today. I'm sure you want your mistress to have her wits about her for a meeting that will decide both our fates—don't' you?

PERSUASION: Yes, mistress.

APHRODITE: Now, you remember what you're supposed to do?

PERSUASION: This cup for Artemis and this one for Hera...

APHRODITE: And this one, with the *water*, for me. And then, after today, neither Artemis nor Hera shall ever rule the hearts of women again, for I, Aphrodite, Goddess of Love and Delight, shall control the culture, and the goddess who controls the culture shall also rule the hearts, the minds, the souls, and the bodies of women.

PERSUASION: But how will you control the culture?

APHRODITE: I shall control the woman who creates the culture.

PERSUASION: You don't mean—

APHRODITE: Oh, but I do! Sappho! The legendary poet of Lesbos. After today, every Lesbian shall be taught to kneel at my sacred cleft and drink of my cyprian nectar! *(Raising the decanter exultantly.)*

PERSUASION: Mistress, here come the goddesses! *(ARTEMIS and HERA enter. ARTEMIS is wearing a tunic of bearskins, and HERA is dressed in a matronly outfit.)*

ARTEMIS: *(Saluting.)* Hail, Aphrodite!

APHRODITE: Artemis. How nice to see you again. *(Sniffing the bearskin.)* Persuasion, would you light the incense, please. *(PERSUASION is staring at ARTEMIS.)* Persuasion!

PERSUASION: *(Jolting to attention.)* Yes, mistress!

ARTEMIS: *(Contemptuously.)* Your slave certainly knows her place.

APHRODITE: *(Smiling.)* She loves her work.

ARTEMIS: The work of a panderer for a pimp!

APHRODITE: *(Deliberately ignoring the remark.)* Ah, Hera... How nice to see you again.

HERA: *(Hugging her.)* Aphrodite. It's been too long.

APHRODITE: Yes, it's a pity there should be such a distance between the Goddess of Marriage and the Goddess of Love.

ARTEMIS: The "Goddess of Lust" would be more apt.

APHRODITE: *(Turning to ARTEMIS.)* Perhaps, Artemis, the distinction has become blurred by your keeping so much company with the bears.

ARTEMIS: There is more dignity in the crudest animal mating ritual than in all the so-called sacred rites of your decadent cult, Aphrodite!

APHRODITE: You might have more credibility if you could speak from experience.

ARTEMIS: I don't need to put my hand in the fire to know that it burns.

APHRODITE: *(Vamping her.)* But just how close do you have to come to feel the heat? *(ARTEMIS pulls away in shock. APHRODITE laughs, turns away, and claps her hands for her slave.)* Persuasion! Please, some refreshments for our visitors!

ARTEMIS: *(To PERSUASION.)* Do you always do what you're told?

PERSUASION: The greatest freedom is in the service of love.

ARTEMIS: Love! You can't believe desire has anything to do with love!

PERSUASION: *(Blushing.)* For me it does.

ARTEMIS: Then you deserve your chains. *(PERSUASION is mortified.)*

APHRODITE: Persuasion—you will serve the drinks!

PERSUASION: Yes, mistress. *(She turns her back to APHRODITE to pick up the tray.)*

ARTEMIS: You know I never touch your nectar.

APHRODITE: Yes, of course. Persuasion has arranged for a special cup of spring water for you—haven't you, Persuasion? *(PERSUASION has dumped out the contents of ARTEMIS's cup and is busy pouring the contents of APHRODITE's cup into ARTEMIS's. She refills APHRODITE's cup with nectar.)* Persuasion?

PERSUASION: *(Turning.)* Yes, mistress?

APHRODITE: I was telling Artemis how you have arranged to serve her spring water. Isn't that true?

PERSUASION: Oh, yes! I swear!

APHRODITE: *(To ARTEMIS.)* You see? *(To PERSUASION.)* Now, will you serve our guests, please? *(PERSUASION hands a cup to HERA.)*

HERA: Well, I hope that *mine* is nectar. You know how I love it. So delicate, and yet so…

APHRODITE: Commanding.

HERA: *(Toasting.)* Yes! *(HERA drains the contents in one draught. Meanwhile, ARTEMIS has turned her back on PERSUASION.)*

APHRODITE: Persuasion, why haven't you served our Arcadian friend? *(HERA pours herself another cup.)*

PERSUASION: She won't let me.

ARTEMIS: Artemis shall never be attended by a slave.

APHRODITE: Then allow me to serve you myself. Or does it hurt your pride to be waited on by a goddess? *(Handing ARTEMIS the cup which PERSUASION has filled with spring water)* And now, a toast! *(Taking her own cup, now filled with nectar.)* To youth and beauty!

HERA: *(Giggling.)* To wisdom and maturity! *(Hiccup.)*

ARTEMIS: To sobriety and self-reliance! *(They drink. Suddenly APHRODITE spits out a mouthful of nectar.)*

APHRODITE: Persuasion!

PERSUASION: *(Terrified.)* Mistress?

APHRODITE: Did you do as I ordered?

PERSUASION: Yes, mistress.

APHRODITE: *(Throwing the contents of her cup in PERSUASION's face.)* Liar! Traitor!

HERA: *(Shocked.)* What did she do?

APHRODITE: *(Enraged.)* She knows what she has done. *(She crosses to PERSUASION as if to strike her.)*

ARTEMIS: *(Stepping between them.)* Aphrodite—strike that woman and you'll answer to me.

HERA: What did she do? *(She pours herself another cup.)*

APHRODITE: Persuasion, we'll discuss this later. Now, go! *(PERSUASION exits, and APHRODITE turns to her guests.)* I apologize for my slave. Shall we get on with the business of the meeting?

HERA: *(Starting to pour again.)* Just one more teeny—

ARTEMIS: We didn't come here to drink.

HERA: *(Ashamed, she sets the decanter down.)* No, of course not—*(Hiccup.)*

ARTEMIS: We came here to discuss the situation on Lesbos.

HERA: Why don't you start? *(Furtively, she refills her goblet.)*

ARTEMIS: Well, as we all know, Sappho's school for young women on the island of Lesbos has become the most famous of the civilized world, and Sappho is training the artists—the dancers, the singers, the poets, the playwrights—who will influence the culture of all Greece. The culture of Lesbos shall determine the culture of women, and the culture of women shall determine the culture of the Western world. And so, Hera and I have wearied of our rivalries with you for the heart of this Lesbian, and we would decide, here and now, once and for all, which one shall be her goddess—because as it is, she wars against herself, and the students are led this way one day and that way the next—and all of Lesbos is in upheaval.

HERA: *(Cutting in, drunk.)* Marriage. Every woman needs the protection of marriage.

ARTEMIS: I have come here today to present my arguments—

HERA: *(Interrupting.)* It doesn't have to be with men. Women can marry women. As long as they are faithful. That is the main thing. As long as they are faithful. As long as they don't do it with anyone except their partner. Even if they don't do it anymore with their partner—as long as it's always the same partner they don't do it with—

APHRODITE: *(Cutting her off.)* And your arguments, Artemis?

ARTEMIS: My argument is that every woman must learn to love herself, and if she did that, there would be no need for temples to Aphrodite or to Hera, because she would not need the intoxication of romance or the slavery of marriage in order to feel her self-worth. The women who worship at my altar find they worship at their own.

APHRODITE: Oh, Artemis, you have such a pole up your ass! *(HERA giggles and ARTEMIS glares at her.)* The world—say what you will— is very banal, and life is very tedious, and if it weren't for Aphrodite and her nectar, how many women do you think would ever hear the mermaids sing? How many women would go to their graves never knowing the poetry of their own souls, the music of that most glorious instrument of love—a veritable lyre, as it were, that quivers as the gentle—and may I say, expert— fingering of Aphrodite sets up that rich vibration which will not be "diminuendo" until every cadence, every contour has been sounded, until every cavity reverberates with the hum, the murmur, the ululation, the moan, the howl, the roar, the crescendo "passionata" of one grand syncophonous concatenation! Or perhaps I should liken it more to the delicate strains of the aeolian harp— yes—that more subtle instrument whose only fingering is the soft and stirring breeze which teases itself across the taut and arching strings as they offer themselves up to the fickle evening air—to the torment of playful zephyrs who flurry them with tuneless melodies the livelong night, and then skip carelessly away at the light of dawn, abandoning the still-straining strings to the quivering agonies of their merciless cantata sans finale. *(APHRODITE collapses from her exertions.)*

ARTEMIS: *(Unimpressed.)* And how many women will pay for your nectar with a lifetime of addiction, pining and sighing and groveling at your altar for another taste—*(A figure in a cloak approaches the altar. She carries a scroll.)*

APHRODITE: Oh, look! Here comes one of my worshippers now!

ARTEMIS: One of your slaves!

APHRODITE: Why, it's Sappho herself!

HERA: *(Rising drunkenly.)* Hail, Sappho!

ARTEMIS: Sit down, Hera. You know the mortals can't see us.

SAPPHO: *(She unrolls the scroll and reads.)*

> *"Aphrodite, beauty of the skies,*
> *To whom a thousand temples rise,*
> *Gaily false in gentle smiles,*
> *Full of love-perplexing wiles;*
> *O goddess, from my heart remove*
> *The wasting cares and pains of love.*
>
> *Though now she shuns thy longing arms,*
> *She soon shall court thy slighted charms...*
> *Though now she freeze, she soon shall burn,*
> *And be thy victim in her turn...*
> *Favour thy suppliant's hidden fires,*
> *And give me all my heart desires."*

(At the end, SAPPHO presents the scroll for an offering on the altar. She exits. APHRODITE takes the scroll.)

APHRODITE: Wasn't that charming? Souvenir? *(Offering it to ARTEMIS.)*

ARTEMIS: *(Disdaining the scroll.)* It seems she wants her girlfriend back.

APHRODITE: *(Smiling.)* Yes.

HERA: Wait! I know! It's Gongyla! That's her girlfriend. Gongyla is one of *my* followers. She has been praying to me for Sappho to marry her. She has a daughter, you see, and she doesn't want the little girl to be exposed to Sappho's infidelities. And so Gongyla has left Sappho, because Sappho will not promise to be monogamous... Oh, if only Sappho would pray at my temple, I could fix everything!

ARTEMIS: If Sappho would pray at my temple, she would learn about her self-worth, and then she would not have to be such a slave to sex.

APHRODITE: Ah but, girls— she prays to me. And I, Aphrodite, Goddess of Love, shall answer! Persuasion! *(PERSUASION enters, shame-faced.)* Persuasion... Yes, you should be ashamed. We'll talk about your behavior

11

later. But right now I need you to go down to Lesbos, to Sappho's school, and I want you to get the student named Atthis and send her to Sappho's bedchamber tonight.

HERA: But what about Gongyla?

ARTEMIS: Atthis! Not Atthis, the runner? *(APHRODITE smiles.)* She's one of *my* followers—a celibate!

APHRODITE: *(To PERSUASION.)* Send her tonight.
ARTEMIS: Don't you dare!

APHRODITE: *(To PERSUASION.)* You heard me!

ARTEMIS: *(Stopping PERSUASION.)* Would you prostitute an innocent young woman? Would you sell her into a lifetime of sexual addiction?

APHRODITE: Persuasion, go!

ARTEMIS: Panderer!

PERSUASION: *(To ARTEMIS.)* I have no choice!

ARTEMIS: You always have a choice.

APHRODITE: *Go! (PERSUASION runs out.)*

ARTEMIS: Aphrodite, I won't forgive you for this.

APHRODITE: If you can't hold onto your followers, Artemis, it's not my fault. Perhaps the celibate life is not all it's cracked up to be.

ARTEMIS: You know Persuasion uses *nectar* to seduce. Yes, nectar, that poisonous drug that destroys the minds of women, turning them into helpless addicts with only one idea, one fixation, one obsession in life—nectar, nectar, nectar! *(She pours the decanter's contents over the table.)*

HERA: Oh, no! No! What have you done? *(HERA tries to soak up the nectar with her scarf and then wring it into her cup. She ends by lapping the nectar from the table.)*

ARTEMIS: And this is our Goddess of Marriage— reduced to servile groveling for a taste of romance in order to make her slavery more palatable!

12

No, Aphrodite, I've had enough of polite games. This is war. I shall win Sappho away from you, and I shall do it without drugs, without magic.

APHRODITE: *(Amused.)* And just how do you propose to do that?

ARTEMIS: I propose to adopt a mortal form and set up a school on Lesbos to rival Sappho's—a school where young women will learn the skills to take care of themselves in the wild, and when Sappho sees how her students prefer the wholesome and empowering teachings of my school to the decadent dissipations of hers— then she will abandon the temple of Aphrodite and devote herself to the following of Artemis.
APHRODITE: I see.

ARTEMIS: Indeed—and so you shall! You and your slavish followers will be banished from Lesbos forever, and the Goddess of Marriage shall find that without your nectar, her temples are deserted! *(She exits abruptly. APHRODITE turns back to HERA, who is still soaking up nectar.)*

APHRODITE: Oh, for Gaia's sake, Hera— stop that! Here, take the whole bottle! *(She hands her the decanter.)*

BLACKOUT

END OF SCENE

ACT I

SCENE 2

Lights come up on SAPPHO's bedchamber on Lesbos. It is the sleeping quarters of a practicing Lesbian poet. The time is just before dawn, and the room is still dim. SAPPHO, a handsome butch woman in her early forties, is on her bed, trying to write a poem. She has been writing all night.

SAPPHO: *(Composing.)*

> *"No more... no more!*
> *Impossible to move*
> *A hardened heart... "*

(Sighing.) No, I don't mean that! Gongyla is not hard-hearted. Soft-hearted. Soft... so soft.

> *"... And I will set you...*
> *...reclining...*
> *...on soft pillows... "*

(Sighing.) New pillows. It will take more than new pillows to get her to come back this time. *(Looking out the window.)*

> *"O, not the honey...*
> *Or the bee!"*

(There is a knock at the door, and SAPPHO throws down the poems.) It's Gongyla! It's Gongyla! She's come back! Thank you, Aphrodite! Thank you, thank you, thank you! I knew you would answer my prayer! *(She crosses to the door.)* Oh, thank you, Aphrodite! *(She opens the door. ATTHIS, 18, a "baby butch," stands at the door.)* Atthis.

ATTHIS: Sappho?

SAPPHO: Atthis, what do you want?

ATTHIS: I was wondering if I could talk to you.

SAPPHO: It's early. The sun isn't even up yet!

ATTHIS: I know, but I couldn't sleep, and I saw your lamp burning...

14

SAPPHO: I was working on a poem.

ATTHIS: Oh, then I don't want to bother you. *(She turns to go.)*

SAPPHO: *(Sighing.)* No, that's all right. Would you like to hear it?

ATTHIS: Oh, yes. I love your poetry.

SAPPHO:

> *"O, not the honey...*
> *Or the bee!"*

(ATTHIS bursts into tears.) Well, I knew there was a problem with the meter, but I didn't think it was that bad.

ATTHIS: No, I'm crying because it made me think of Anactoria.

SAPPHO: Anactoria? Oh, your little friend from Lydia. The two of you grew up together, didn't you? *(ATTHIS snuffles.)* And then your parents sent you both here to study with me... *(Another snuffle.)* And now you're crying, because Anactoria's parents have picked out a soldier for her to marry, and the day after tomorrow, she will be leaving Lesbos to sail back to the mainland for the wedding.

ATTHIS: *(Sobbing.)* Yes.

SAPPHO: That's hard, isn't it?

ATTHIS: She's my best friend.

SAPPHO: Well, there will be other girls—other best friends.

ATTHIS: I don't want anyone else except her.

SAPPHO: I know the feeling, but sometimes things just don't work out that way.

ATTHIS: Isn't there something I can do to stop her—to make her see that she belongs with me, that marrying this man is going to be the worst mistake of her life?

SAPPHO: She loves her parents?

ATTHIS: She says she does, but I think she's just afraid of them.

SAPPHO: Let her go, Atthis. Let her go.

ATTHIS: But isn't there *something* I can do? I know she loves me.

SAPPHO: But does *she* know it?

ATTHIS: That's the thing. How can I make her know it? How can I show her that I'm the one she loves?

SAPPHO: Have you told her?

ATTHIS: Yes, yes! I've told her. A hundred times. And I've written poems— and sung them to her!

SAPPHO: Have you kissed her?

ATTHIS: Of course.

SAPPHO: You have? Like what? Show me.

ATTHIS: Like this. *(She kisses SAPPHO on the cheek.)*

SAPPHO: I see.

ATTHIS: What? Is there something wrong with that?

SAPPHO: Well, that's not the kind of kiss I was thinking of.

ATTHIS: There's another kind?

SAPPHO: There are thousands of other kinds.

ATTHIS: And you think they would make her call off the marriage?

SAPPHO: Stranger things have happened.

ATTHIS: Show me those kisses!

SAPPHO: All of them?

ATTHIS: Just the best ones.

SAPPHO: I'll show you *one*. Now relax. Relax your shoulders. Pretend you're Anactoria, and I'm you. And you tell her to close her eyes... Now, close your eyes.

ATTHIS: But then I won't be able to see!

SAPPHO: You'll feel it. Close your eyes. *(ATTHIS closes her eyes.)* And then you start with her shoulder, very lightly—like this... *(SAPPHO kisses ATTHIS' bare arm.)* And you work your way up to her neck... *(Working up to her neck.)*... And you kiss her right in the hollow of her neck here—like this... *(Kissing the hollow.)*

ATTHIS: *(Opening her eyes.)* My heart's pounding like I just ran a mile. What does that mean?

SAPPHO: Close your eyes. It means it's working. *(ATTHIS closes her eyes.)* And then you kiss her ears. And you take the very tip of your tongue and trace the curves around inside her ear—slowly, until you get right to the center, like this...

ATTHIS: *(Her eyes fly open.)* Oh!

SAPPHO: What?

ATTHIS: I felt it.

SAPPHO: Yes?

ATTHIS: But not in my ear. You'll never believe where I felt it.

SAPPHO: Yes, I would. Now, close your eyes. *(ATTHIS closes her eyes.)* And then you take her face in your hands—gently—and you kiss her eyelids... *(Kissing her eyelids.)*... and her nose... *(Kissing her nose.)*... and her chin... *(Kissing her chin.)*

ATTHIS: *(Breathless, eyes closed.)* And then?

SAPPHO: And then you press your lips so softly against hers she'll think she's dreaming, and you hold them there until you feel her lips separate a little, and then you take the tip of your tongue, like this... *(SAPPHO gives ATTHIS a long, sexy kiss.)*

ATTHIS: *(Eyes closed.)* Oh, oh! My heart! My head! Oh!

SAPPHO: And that is one way to kiss a woman you love.

ATTHIS: And you say there are thousands of other ways?

SAPPHO: At least.

ATTHIS: Oh, goddess! Oh, goddess! Show me!

SAPPHO: Not now. I want you to practice that one—

ATTHIS: Okay! *(She reaches for SAPPHO, who pulls back.)*

SAPPHO:… on your girlfriend.

ATTHIS: Shouldn't I try it out on you first?

SAPPHO: You'll do fine. Now, I need to get back to my poem.

ATTHIS: Oh, yeah. Well, I'll let you know how it goes.

SAPPHO: You do that.

ATTHIS: Thanks, Sappho! *(Rising, she heads for the door, but she turns suddenly.)*
Oh—You must have spilled something on your bed, because I sat on something wet—

SAPPHO: *(Cutting her off.)* Go back to bed, Atthis. *(SAPPHO closes the door. She turns back to her poetry, smiling and shaking her head.)*

BLACKOUT

END OF SCENE

ACT I

SCENE 3

Lights come up on Aphrodite's temple. It's the same morning; the sun is up. This is the same party from the first scene, except the goblets, etc., have been cleared. HERA is lying down with an ice pack on her head. APHRODITE is raging.

APHRODITE: I can't believe it! She kissed the young woman once and sent her back to bed—alone! *(Crossing to HERA.)* This isn't like Sappho! She's never turned down a student before! And the woman was ready—she was begging for it! I can't understand it!

HERA: I told you—Sappho is really in love with Gongyla.

APHRODITE: Don't be ridiculous.

HERA: Say what you will, but as a woman gets older, she starts looking for something more than passion in her relationships.

APHRODITE: *(Irritated.)* I know that.

HERA: *(Half sitting.)* You do?

APHRODITE: Of course. She looks for technique. But the girl was teachable!

HERA: Aphrodite, I don't understand why we can't be allies. Why can't we share Sappho?

APHRODITE: You're joking, aren't you?

HERA: No. I don't see why Sappho can't marry Gongyla and still be one of your worshippers.

APHRODITE: Because desire and commitment make strange bedfellows.

HERA: But why?

APHRODITE: *(Impatient.)* Because mystery is the essence of desire, and you know perfectly well there's nothing mysterious about a person who lives with you... except why. Have some more nectar. It does wonders for a hangover. *(Clapping her hands, as HERA pours herself a drink.)* Persuasion! Where is

19

that girl? I sent her to seduce Sappho, not have her teach kissing lessons! Persuasion! This is twice she has disobeyed me. *Persuasion*!

PERSUASION: *(Appearing suddenly, all innocence.)* Yes, mistress?

APHRODITE: *(Imitating her.)* "Yes, mistress?" Oh, don't try your little tricks on me, my girl. Remember, I'm the one who taught you all of them. Why didn't you do as I commanded?

PERSUASION: *(Wide-eyed.)* I did.

APHRODITE: Oh, you did?

PERSUASION: Yes, Mistress.

APHRODITE: I see. And what was it I commanded?

PERSUASION: You told me to send Atthis to Sappho, and that's what I did.

APHRODITE: You slippery little liar! You knew perfectly well I meant for you to arrange a seduction, not a pajama party!

PERSUASION: That wasn't what you said.

APHRODITE: And I suppose you have no idea how the nectar got into my cup?

PERSUASION: Maybe the cups got mixed up.

APHRODITE: The only thing that got mixed up was a certain little slave girl. *(She slaps PERSUASION.)*

HERA: *(Frightened.)* I'm sure she meant no harm—did you, dear?

APHRODITE: Oh, no harm at all. She only meant to make a fool out of her mistress! Isn't that right? *(PERSUASION hides behind HERA.)* Did you know that my little slave girl has a crush on Artemis? Isn't that precious? *(To PERSUASION.)* Maybe you should petition Hera to do a little matchmaking for you. I'm sure the great Artemis wouldn't mind at all marrying an ignorant little slave girl. I'm sure the Goddess of Celibacy would be fascinated by all your little arts of seduction. What was it she called you? "Panderer," wasn't it? Of course, you might have to serve Artemis my nectar in order to seduce her... oh, I forgot! That's the part where you switched the cups, wasn't it? *(She takes another swing at PERSUASION who ducks behind HERA.)* Well, just see how far your little romance gets without my nectar! Just see if Artemis—or anyone else for that matter—would even look at you without my nectar! You're not pretty, you know. In fact, you're really very ugly. *(Changing tack.)* But maybe Hera would have a use for a disobedient little slave girl...?

HERA: *(Quickly.)* Oh, slavery is against the principles of marriage.

APHRODITE: Since when? *(Turning back to PERSUASION.)* Well, I guess we'll just have to find some other appropriate method of discipline... Ah! I have it! Your favorite goddess is currently on Lesbos, passing herself off as a mortal teacher. Why don't we just send you down the mountain to be one of her students?

PERSUASION: *(Panicked.)* No!

APHRODITE: *(Smiling.)* Yes, I think that's just the place for you—the perfect opportunity for you to learn about the joys of abstinence and deprivation—

PERSUASION: No, mistress, please! I'll do anything—anything you want but please don't send me down to Lesbos! I'll do anything, go anywhere, be anybody—just please, please, don't make me go live with the Lesbians!

APHRODITE: Silence! You will go to Lesbos and you will enroll yourself in Artemis' school.

PERSUASION: But—

APHRODITE: Silence! Go—and you are not to return until I send for you.

PERSUASION: But—

APHRODITE: GO! *(PERSUASION exits.)*

HERA: Don't you think that might have been a bit too harsh?

APHRODITE: It's good for her. She'll come running back. Wait and see. A few hours of gutting deer carcasses and digging latrines, and she'll be begging me to take her back. Have some more nectar. *(Pouring HERA a drink.)*
HERA: *(Uncomfortable.)* No, I don't think so.

APHRODITE: What? Are you refusing to drink my nectar?

HERA: Yes. Yes, I believe I am. *(She turns and exits with tipsy dignity, leaving APHRODITE holding the cup.)*

APHRODITE: *(To audience.)* Well, this is quite a twist, isn't it? The Slave of Love, a celibate, and the Goddess of Marriage a teetotaler. Well, neither one of them will get very far without me. But let them try. *(Taking a drink.)* Yes, let them try!

BLACKOUT

END OF SCENE

ACT I

SCENE 4

The same morning. Lights come up on Hera's temple at Lesbos. The city of Mytilene is visible in the distance. GONGYLA, a feminine woman in her mid-thirties, is kneeling in prayer in front of a basket filled with scrolls.

GONGYLA: Oh, Hera, great wife and mother, hear the plea of your humble follower, Gongyla. Here, here on your altar, at your temple on Lesbos, I make the greatest sacrifice of my life to you—Here! Here are the songs of Sappho, all of the love poems she ever wrote for me when she was my lover. *(She breaks down weeping.)* Oh, Hera, I loved her. I loved her so much. I'll always love her. And yet I know it was not a love that was pleasing to you. It wasn't pleasing to me! Sappho was always leaving me to chase after her students. Could anything have been more humiliating? And the excuses I made for her! "She can't help herself, because she was an orphan..." "She is only trying to give those young women the love she never had..." An excuse for every infidelity. And always I thought if I could just be more tolerant and understanding, she would eventually tire of these endless dramas and settle down and marry me. Oh, Hera, what a fool I have been! And you have been so patient with me and all my prayers—prayers for you to change Sappho's heart! But Sappho's goddess is Aphrodite, and Aphrodite alone rules her unruly heart. And so now, finally, the long and stormy night of passion and betrayal is over. And in the cold grey dawn of resolution, there is nothing but a vast sea of emptiness—and this quiet wreck that used to be my heart. *(Placing the basket on the altar.)* Hera, I make this sacrifice of my love at your altar—I offer you my dreams of marriage to Sappho, and in return I ask only this: that you give me the strength to live without her, for my sake and for the sake of my daughter Cleis.

(She bows her head, turning her back to the audience. GORGO, a butch in her mid-thirties, enters holding CLEIS by the hand. CLEIS is about six. GORGO motions for CLEIS to be quiet. She sneaks up behind GONGYLA and puts her hands over her eyes.)

GONGYLA: Oh! Who is it?

CLEIS: Guess, Mommy!

GONGYLA: Well… it's not Cleis, because your hands aren't this big.

CLEIS: Guess! Guess!

23

GONGYLA: And… it's not Grandma, because her hands aren't as warm as these…

CLEIS: Guess!

GONGYLA: Well… it's not Cleis, and it's not Grandmother—

CLEIS: *(Interrupting.)* And it's not Sappho!

GORGO: *(Bitterly.)* No, it's not Sappho.

GONGYLA: *(Taking down the hands gently.)* It's Gorgo.

CLEIS: No fair! You recognized her voice!

GORGO: *(To GONGYLA.)* Are you disappointed?

GONGYLA: That you didn't let me guess?

GORGO: That it wasn't Sappho.

GONGYLA: Cleis, honey, go pick Mommy some wild oleanders, and she'll make you a wreath for your hair. Like the women wear at Thesmophoria… .remember? Go on! *(CLEIS exits.)*

GORGO: Are you wishing I was Sappho?

GONGYLA: Gorgo, why do you keep asking me that? You know I'm not seeing her anymore.

GORGO: Your eyes are wet from crying. You still love her.

GONGYLA: Even the hardiest oak will weep when a branch is torn from its trunk. I can't help what I feel.

GORGO: Why can't you feel that love for me?

GONGYLA: Gorgo, it's too soon. Give me time. Sappho and I were together for so many years.

GORGO: Together! You mean when Sappho wasn't with her other girlfriends.

GONGYLA: *(Looking down.)* There's no point in hurting me with the past, Gorgo. It's done, and I've left her.

GORGO: But you'll go back. You have before.

GONGYLA: *(Shaking her head.)* Not any more. I was younger, and scared, because I was alone with Cleis, and she was just a baby. But now I'm older, and Cleis is not so dependent—and neither am I. I can't allow myself to be treated like that any more, and I don't want Cleis to grow up with that kind of example. She's getting old enough to understand.

GORGO: *(Taking GONGYLA's hands.)* So will you marry me? *(GONGYLA looks down.)* I have inherited my father's shipping business. I own a big house—big enough for Cleis to have her own room—and everything she could want. She'll never be hungry or cold, and I can love her. You know Sappho never had time for her.

GONGYLA: It's true.

GORGO: Marry me, Gongyla. Let me be the family you want. I love you. And I love Cleis.

GONGYLA: It's too soon.

GORGO: Then let me court you. *(Taking her hands again.)* Please. Just let me see you. There's a meteor shower tonight… Why don't you have dinner with me, and we can watch it together?

GONGYLA: I don't know…

GORGO: Wait! I have a better idea! We can have a picnic at Aphrodite's temple, on the cliffs. The view would be even better. And you could bring Cleis, if she's allowed to stay up that late…

GONGYLA: *(Smiling.)* Oh, she would love that.

GORGO: May I ask her?

GONGYLA: *(Smiling.)* Go ahead. She's off picking oleanders. *(GORGO exits, and GONGYLA watches her. SAPPHO enters quietly and stands behind her. She holds out a poem. GONGYLA turns with a start.)* Sappho! *(Looking at the scroll.)* What's this?

SAPPHO: A poem.

GONGYLA: I don't want any more of your poems.

SAPPHO: Read it. *(GONGYLA refuses to take it.)* Then I'll read it to you:

> *"Come tonight with your Lydian lyre,*
> *Come, rosebud mine; this heart's desire,*
> *Sweet Gongyla, must go out to you,*
> *For glimpse of your gown hath filled me through*
> *And put new joy in my heart.*
> *I too found fault once on a day*
> *With the Lady of Love—whose grace I pray*
> *These words of mine may not lose for me,*
> *But bring me a maid I'd rather see*
> *Than all her kind apart."*

GONGYLA: Sappho...

SAPPHO: That's one of my favorites. Like this gown. *(Tracing the neck of GONGYLA's gown.)*

GONGYLA: What are you doing here?

SAPPHO: Here? *(Referring to GONGYLA's cleavage.)*

GONGYLA: At Hera's temple. *(Removing her hand.)* Since when did you have any use for the Goddess of Marriage?

SAPPHO: It's a place of public worship, isn't it? Or maybe women with my reputation aren't welcome...

GONGYLA: I thought Aphrodite was your goddess.

SAPPHO: *(Close to her ear.)* You used to like that.

GONGYLA: *(Eyes down.)* Sappho, what do you want?

SAPPHO: *(With passionate intensity.)* You know what I want. No one has ever known so well what I want. *(She puts her hands on the side of GONGYLA's breasts.)*

GONGYLA: *(Removing them.)* Don't.

SAPPHO: *(Kissing her hands.)* I miss you. All I do is write poems about you...

GONGYLA: Stop!

SAPPHO: You don't want me to.

GONGYLA: *(Rising.)* Yes, I do. Sappho, I want a home, a marriage. I want a partner I can trust. *(GORGO enters with CLEIS, who has the flowers.)*

GORGO: Oh, I didn't realize you had company.

GONGYLA: I don't. I mean...

SAPPHO: She means I was just leaving. Nice to see you again, Gorgo. Did you ever get over that woman Dika?

GORGO: Very nicely. In fact, you did me a favor by seducing her. *(Turning to GONGYLA.)* Cleis is very excited about the picnic... *(Turning to CLEIS.)*... aren't you? *(To GONGYLA.)* So, I'll meet you both at sunset—at Aphrodite's temple. *(Turning back to SAPPHO.)* Oh, Sappho, be sure to catch the meteor shower tonight. Quite a sight when the stars themselves fall from the heavens. *(She exits.)*

SAPPHO: You're meeting Gorgo at Aphrodite's temple? What's this—your new girlfriend? Couldn't you even wait a week?

GONGYLA: Oh, Sappho, I've waited five years! And at least I bothered to break up before I started dating!

SAPPHO: You've done well for yourself—Gorgo is one of the wealthiest women on the island.

GONGYLA: You know I don't care about that.

SAPPHO: Still, it must be a pleasant change after being lovers with a woman who has had to work to support herself all her life—

GONGYLA: Sappho—

SAPPHO: I'll bet Gorgo has never had to live in the homes of strangers, to depend on their charity—

GONGYLA: I'm not interested in her money.

SAPPHO: But you *are* interested.

GONGYLA: I didn't say that!

CLEIS: Mommy, look! Here's the flowers.

GONGYLA: Let's go home, Cleis. I'll braid them there.

SAPPHO: *(Trying to intercept CLEIS.)* Let's see, Cleis.

CLEIS: No! These are mine!

GONGYLA: Come on, honey… Let's go.

(SAPPHO stands for a moment watching them depart, then she turns towards HERA's altar. She notices the scrolls for the first time, and recognizes that they are her poems. In a rage, she gathers them up and exits.)

BLACKOUT

END OF SCENE

ACT I

SCENE 5

Lights come up on APHRODITE's temple on Lesbos, the same morning. APHRODITE enters and begins pacing.

APHRODITE: Very clever, Hera... very clever—getting Gongyla to break up with Sappho and then setting her up with Gorgo. Very clever. Because we both know, if there's one thing that Sappho can't resist, it's a woman who is unavailable. Why, she might even become desperate enough to commit marriage. Yes, Hera, that was very, very clever. Frankly, I wouldn't have expected it of you... *(Pouring herself a cup of nectar.)* But if you think you can beat me at my own game, my little goddess of happy-ever-after, then you are very much mistaken! You and Artemis and Persuasion—that unfaithful girl!—you all think you can outwit me with you little intrigues, but you are nothing but amateurs! Do you hear me? *Amateurs!(Lifting the glass.)* Yes, you may have my queen in check, Hera—Check... but not mate! *(She tips back her head and drinks with abandon.)*

BLACKOUT

END OF SCENE

ACT I

SCENE 6

Lights come up on HERA's temple at Lesbos. It's high noon. There is a circle of young women who are practicing a choral work. These are SAPPHO'S STUDENTS. A young woman, ANACTORIA, stands in the center of the circle.

STUDENTS: *(Chanting.)*

> *"O beautiful, O charming one,*
> *With thee sport*
> *The rosy-ankled Graces*
> *And golden Aprhodite."*

FIRST GIRL: Wait... wait! Anactoria is supposed to be blindfolded.

ANACTORIA: Who says I am?

FIRST GIRL: Gongyla. She said that's how they did it the last time Sappho's "Wedding Songs" were performed on Lesbos.

ANACTORIA: But why?

SECOND GIRL: So she can't see what her husband looks like until it's too late. *(The young women laugh.)*

THIRD GIRL: Have you ever seen him, Anactoria?

ANACTORIA: No, but my parents have.

SECOND GIRL: Naked? *(They all giggle.)*

ANACTORIA: You are all such babies. Come on, let's rehearse this. We have to perform it tomorrow when my parents get here.

FIRST GIRL: What if he's hideously ugly?

ANACTORIA: He's very tall and handsome.

SECOND GIRL: You hope!

FIRST GIRL: Better get her the blindfold.

30

ANACTORIA: Well, I don't see the point—

SECOND GIRL: No, but you'll feel it on the wedding night! *(The young women laugh.)*

ANACTORIA: *(Disgusted.)* Give me your scarf! *(She ties it on herself as a blindfold.)* Come on, I want to get through the rehearsal. I have to pack tonight. Let's go.

SECOND GIRL: She already sounds like her mother!

ANACTORIA: Let's go!

STUDENTS: *(Chanting.)*

"O beautiful, O charming one,
With thee sport
The rosy-ankled Graces
And golden Aphrodite."

ANACTORIA: *(Chanting.)*

"Do I still long for maidenhood?"

STUDENTS:

"Ye rosy-armed, pure Graces, come,
Daughters of Zeus, be near!"

(Three young women step forward and link arms. They begin to circle around ANACTORIA. As they chant the Hymenaon, they raise their arms and then lower them, still circling. The outer circle begins to circle in the opposite direction.)

"Up with the rafters high,
Ho for the wedding!
Raise them high, carpenters,
Ho for the wedding!
The bridegroom's as tall as Ares,
Ho for the wedding!
Far taller than a tall man,
Ho for the wedding!
Towering as the Lesbian poet,
Ho for the wedding!

Over the poets of other lands,
Ho for the wedding!

(The circles break apart to form two rows, revealing ATTHIS at their head, dressed as a bridegroom.)

Thou happy bridegroom! Now has dawned
That day of days supreme,
When in thine arms, thou'll hold at last
The maiden of thy dream.

(The women begin to pull and shove ANACTORIA towards ATTHIS.)

Bride, around whom the rosy loves are flying,
Sweet image of Aphrodite undying,
The bed awaits thee; go, and with him lying,
Give to the groom thy sweetness, softly sighing
May Hesperus in gladness pass before thee,
And Hera of the silver throne bend o'er thee."

ANACTORIA: *(Resisting them.)*

"Maidenhood! Maidenhood! Where
Has thou gone from me,
Whither, O Slain?"

A YOUNG WOMAN: *(Poking and taunting ANACTORIA, who lashes out at her, but misses.)*

"I shall return to thee, I
Who have gone from thee, never again."

(SAPPHO'S STUDENTS run off stage right, stifling their laughter. ATTHIS remains behind.)

ANACTORIA: Well, go on. Where's the second part of "Lament for a Maidenhead?" How does it go? *(Prompting.)*

"Like the sweet apple that reddens..."

Come on!

ATTHIS: *(Reluctantly:)*

"Like the sweet apple that reddens
At the end of the bough—the far end of the bough—
Left by the gatherers swaying, forgotten, so thou.
Nay, not forgotten, ungotten, ungathered till now.

ANACTORIA: Come on! There's another verse...

ATTHIS: *(In pain.)*

Like the wild hyacinth flower, which on the hills is found,
Which the passing feet of the shepherds forever tear and wound,
Until the purple blossom is trodden into the ground."

ANACTORIA: Where's the rest of the chorus? I thought you were all supposed to sing that part... *(Pulling off the blindfold.)* Where is everybody? Where did they go?

ATTHIS: I think it was a joke.

ANACTORIA: Well, it's not very funny. I'm going to tell Sappho. We have to perform this for my parents tomorrow at Hera's temple. Sappho will make them practice. She won't let them ruin her songs. *(She starts to leave.)*

ATTHIS: Anactoria—wait!

ANACTORIA: What?

ATTHIS: *(Embarrassed.)* I... I need to talk to you.

ANACTORIA: Well? *(A pause.)* Atthis, I'm leaving Lesbos tomorrow. I have a lot of things to do to get ready.

ATTHIS: I know. It's about us. About our friendship.

ANACTORIA: What about it?

ATTHIS: Well, I was wondering if you would go with me to Aphrodite's temple.

ANACTORIA: Now?

ATTHIS: It's important.

ANACTORIA: I need to pack. You know I'm sailing tomorrow.

ATTHIS: I know, and I'll never see you again.

ANACTORIA: Yes, you will. Who knows? Your husband might be a soldier from Lydia, too—

ATTHIS: I'm never going to get married.

ANACTORIA: You say that now, but—

ATTHIS: *(Desperate.)* Listen, Tory, you have to come with me right now—to the temple. *(Pulling her.)*

ANACTORIA: Atthis!

ATTHIS: I have to give you something.

ANACTORIA: Give it to me here.

ATTHIS: I can't. I... I made a pledge to the goddess!

ANACTORIA: Oh, Atthis...

ATTHIS: Come on! *(They exit stage left, ATTHIS pulling ANACTORIA. ARTEMIS enters from stage right.)*

ARTEMIS: Gaia! What a band of wild monkeys!—screeching and chattering and running in all directions! Those young women don't need a teacher—they need a trainer! I have never encountered any species so ignorant, so unruly, so *unmanageable* as these Lesbians! All they think about is sex, sex, sex. Thanks to Sappho. She's the one who fills their heads with all this nonsense about romance and love. Her and her poems. Goddess! What a waste of time! When I was their age I was out trapping bears and stalking deer. But not these women! How do they spend their days? Sitting around and writing love songs to each other, holding hands and dancing naked in the meadow, braiding flowers into each other's hair, and then at night—oh, Gaia, don't even get me started on what the Lesbians do at night! *(Lying down on a bench.)* Oh, why did I ever leave the peace and tranquillity of Arcadia for this hornet's nest of Sapphic intrigue? I would rather take on a herd of wild boars than try to teach anything to a young Lesbian! But if I leave now, then Aphrodite wins—and Lesbos is hers. No, I said I would start a rival school on the island, and a rival school I shall start—even if I only have one student. But that one student will have to be a very special young woman—an example for the others . . . A woman who is strong and brave and not afraid to do the things she's never done . . . a woman who is open and honest and someone I can depend on...

Gaia, send me a woman who is modest and unpretentious, a woman who is humble… *(Closing her eyes.)* Like me. *(She falls asleep. PERSUASION enters very quietly, disguised as a Lesbian. She does not see ARTEMIS.)*

PERSUASION: *(To audience.)* Shhh! Don't say anything! It's me, Persuasion! Didn't recognize me, did you? You thought I was a Lesbian, didn't you? Yeah, well, you see, I'm in disguise, because I don't want anyone to know who I am—but especially not Artemis! In fact, I don't even want her to see me! Aphrodite ordered me to come down here and enroll myself as one of her students, but I'm just going to lay low for a few days, until Aphrodite has had time to cool off a little—and then I'll go back, and she'll probably have forgotten the whole thing. Let's face it—the Goddess of Love has a pretty short attention span. *(Pausing.)* But I know what you're thinking. You're thinking it's pretty chickenshit of me to want to go back, especially after telling you how much I hate working for her. That's what you're thinking—and I don't blame you. I said that. I did. And I said that I didn't want to make women fall in love anymore, because I was feeling so bad about how it always turns out. But the truth of the matter is that when you've spent your whole life working for Aphrodite, you don't exactly have a marketable job skills—know what I mean? "Former slave to Goddess of Love seeks employment in related field." Besides, Aphrodite's not so bad—when she's in a good mood. And the benefits are great. No job is perfect, right? *(ARTEMIS turns over, and PERSUASION jumps.)* What's that? Did you hear something? What was it? *(PERSUASION turns and sees ARTEMIS asleep on the bench.)* Oh, Gaia! It's her! It's Artemis! *(Scrambling towards the edge of the stage.)* Oh, goddess, it's her! It's her! *(She leaps into the audience.)* Quick, hide me! Hide me before she sees me! Oh, goddess! Quick! *(Crawling between the seats and over the laps of the audience.)* Hide me! Hide me! *(Suddenly she freezes.)* What am I doing? Why am I acting like such an idiot? This is not a big deal… So I run into a woman I have a crush on— It's not like she's an ax murderer or a collections agent or anything, right? So it's just an incredibly brilliant and attractive woman who happens to be the absolutely most attractive woman on the planet, maybe even the entire universe… ! *(To an audience member.)* It happens to you all the time, doesn't it? You go somewhere and there she is—standing in line next to you, or walking down the street towards you, or maybe she's even sitting in front of you at the theatre. And I bet you don't go crawling under the furniture—do you? No, I bet you just go about your business like there's nothing unusual about the situation. Maybe you even smile at her, like it's no big deal. I mean, it's not your fault that she's a total goddess and you're just a worthless peon. I mean, you can just put your hands in your pockets—if they've been invented yet— and just stroll right on by—like I'm going to do… *(Climbing back onto the stage.)*… I'm just going to walk right on by, just like I didn't even notice she was here. I'm just going to go right on past her… but first, I gotta look at her.

I mean, how often do you get a chance to see a goddess this close up? *(Crossing back to ARTEMIS, who is still asleep.)* Oh, Gaia! Did you ever see anyone so gorgeous in your whole life? I mean, look at those feet! They're so... sensitive. And her breasts! They're so... expressive. And that face... and those lips... Oh, goddess, those lips! *(She leans close to ARTEMIS' face and kisses her lightly. Just then ARTEMIS opens her eyes. She yells, and then PERSUASION yells, and then they both yell together.)*

ARTEMIS: *(Grabbing her bow and nocking an arrow.)* What do you think you're doing?

PERSUASION: I... uh... I—

ARTEMIS: *(She draws the bow, which, for safety's sake, should be strung with loose elastic.)* Well? Speak up!

PERSUASION: I... uh... I—

ARTEMIS: Speak!

PERSUASION: *(Quickly.)* I thought you were someone I knew.

ARTEMIS: *(Scornfully.)* Well, I'm not. I'm not a Lesbian.

PERSUASION: Yes, I can see that now.

ARTEMIS: And a good thing. All you Lesbians can think about is love. *(Eyeing her closely.)* You aren't one of Sappho's students, are you?

PERSUASION: No!

ARTEMIS: Well, that's a point in your favor. *(She lowers the bow.)* What did you say your name was?

PERSUASION: Per—uh, Callisto.

ARTEMIS: Callisto. My name is Andromeda, and I'm new to the island. Maybe you can help me.

PERSUASION: Oh, I don't know anything—

ARTEMIS: I'm starting a school for young women, and I'm looking for students. Would you like me to be your teacher?

PERSUASION: M-m-my teacher?

ARTEMIS: That's right. Would you like me to teach you the skills that will make you a real woman?

PERSUASION: M-m-make me a real woman?

ARTEMIS: *(Pulling PERSUASION down onto the bench with her.)* First, I'd take you out into the woods, and I would show you how to cut and carve a bow, like this one, and then I would teach you how to carve arrows, like these, and then I would teach you how to shoot. And when you knew how to shoot, I would take you up into the hills, where I would teach you how to track the deer. We might be out for days, or even weeks, together—

PERSUASION: W-w-weeks together?

ARTEMIS: That's right. We might have to build a shelter on the side of a mountain, or, if it was a clear night, we could sleep out in the open on the top of a ridge. And then, I would teach you the names of the stars, and I would show you how they travel across the night sky in the different seasons— *(ARTEMIS has put an arm around PERSUASION, and PERSUASION, at the sight of the goddess' hand on her shoulder, faints dead away. ARTEMIS catches her.)* Callisto? Callisto? Are you all right?

PERSUASION: *(Opening her eyes, she sees ARTEMIS and faints again.)* Ohh…

ARTEMIS: Here! Water! *(Cradling the woman, she holds her flask up to PERSUASION's lips. PERSUASION drinks.)* Are you all right?

PERSUASION: I… don't know. What happened?

ARTEMIS: I was telling you about the stars—

PERSUASION: And I started to see them.

ARTEMIS: Are you all right now?

PERSUASION: *(Sighing.)* I've never felt better in my whole life.

ARTEMIS: *(Dropping her.)* Good. Well, I've got to get going. *(She starts to exit.)*

PERSUASION: Wait! *(ARTEMIS turns.)* I thought you wanted to be my teacher?

ARTEMIS: I've changed my mind.

PERSUASION: But why?

ARTEMIS: You faint too much.

PERSUASION: *(Scrambling to her feet.)* No, I don't!

ARTEMIS: Yes, you do.

PERSUASION: No, I don't.

ARTEMIS: Yes, you do!

PERSUASION: Do not!

ARTEMIS: Do too!

PERSUASION: Do not!

ARTEMIS: What am I doing? This is a ridiculous argument!

PERSUASION: No, it isn't.

ARTEMIS: Yes, it is.

PERSUASION: Is not!

ARTEMIS: Is too!

PERSUASION: Is not!

ARTEMIS: I'm leaving!

PERSUASION: Wait! Ar- Andromeda! Just give me a chance… *(ARTEMIS looks at her.)* Please…

ARTEMIS: All right. But just for one day.

PERSUASION: Oh, thank you! Thank you, thank you, thank you! One day! I get to be your slave for one day!

ARTEMIS: My "slave?"

PERSUASION: Student! Student! Did I say "slave?" *(Forcing a laugh.)* Silly me! I get to be your *student*!

ARTEMIS: All right. We better get started. *(She and PERSUASION begin to cross for their exit.)* Now, the most important thing about a woman's bow is the height of it, which depends on her height. What you do is hold your arm out in front of you, like this... *(The women exit as ARTEMIS is explaining about the bow. SAPPHO enters.)*

SAPPHO: All right—where is she? Where is this hayseed of a teacher who is trying to steal my students? I thought the students said she was here, but I don't see anyone. Well, never mind. She can't avoid me for long. Lesbos is a very small island!

BLACKOUT

END OF SCENE

ACT I

SCENE 7

*Lights come up on APHRODITE's temple at Lesbos. It's late
afternoon. APHRODITE, asleep, is sprawled immodestly across the
altar, her hand curled around the decanter. She is snoring. TIMAS
enters. TIMAS is a young woman, eccentrically dressed—what a
more recent culture might call a "nerd," "geek," or "dweeb." Right
off the boat, she carries a bundle of her possessions.*

TIMAS: *(Dumping her bundle, she inspects the temple with reverence. A
mortal, she cannot see APHRODITE.)* I can't believe I'm here—the temple of
Aphrodite! On Lesbos! I'm here! I'm finally here! All those years of reading
Sappho's poems about this place, and I'm finally here! And this... *(Touching
the altar.)*... this is the most sacred of all, the temple of Aphrodite... *(A
particularly loud snore.)*... Queen of Desire, Goddess of all that is lovely,
graceful, and seductive... *(Another snore.)* Priestess of the Poetic... *(Another
snore.)* HAIL APHRODITE!

APHRODITE: *(Sitting up with a snort.)* What the hell? *(She notices her
disarray.)* Damn it! Can't a girl have some privacy?

TIMAS: *(Standing inches from APHRODITE's face, but looking right
through her, as she intones her salutation.)* It is I, Timas of Crete, your
humble worshipper.

APHRODITE: Oh, crap—it's just a mortal. *(She relaxes her efforts to look
impressive and inspects the contents of the decanter, tipping it out. It's
empty.)*

TIMAS: I, Timas, who have just this very hour stepped from the boat that
brought me here, from crossing the watery womb that spawned your
loveliness—

APHRODITE: Get to the point.

TIMAS: And I have come directly here, from the harbor to your temple, to
offer you my humble libation—

APHRODITE: Well, why didn't you say so? *(She holds out a cup.)*

TIMAS: But I shall not insult you with an offering as commonplace as
wine—*(APHRODITE does a long take.)* Oh, no—that would be too cheap.

40

No, the libation I pour for you today shall be no less than a libation from the contents of my own heart —*(APHRODITE pitches the empty goblet over her shoulder.)*... a rare vintage of words plucked from the vineyard of my ripe imagination, trampled with the feet of my brain—

APHRODITE: The "feet" of your brain?

TIMAS:..and fermented in the vats of my own desire—*(APHRODITE does another take.)* OH APHRODITE!

APHRODITE: *(Holding her ears.)* Stop doing that!

TIMAS: Gracious Goddess of Love, I have written this ode to express my gratitude to you for answering my most ardent prayer—

APHRODITE: Refresh my memory.

TIMAS: ... the prayer that my parents would change their minds about Sappho's school, and let me come and live on Lesbos.

APHRODITE: Oh, *that* prayer.

TIMAS: Words can never express what is in my heart today, for without your bountiful help, I might never have known what it meant to be a Lesbian.

APHRODITE: You'll get over it.

TIMAS: So here it is. "Ode to Aphrodite." I hope you like it.

APHRODITE: *(Sourly.)* I can't wait.

TIMAS: *(Clearing her throat, she recites.)*

   "The Queen of Love whose breasts are full,
   Whose hips are round, delect-a-ble!"

APHRODITE: Cronus!

TIMAS:

   "Whose bearded cave holds more delights—"
APHRODITE: "Bearded cave?"

TIMAS: *"Than tongue can praise with heteroclite."*

APHRODITE: "Heteroclite?" What the hell is a heteroclite?

TIMAS:
  "Take me in your wild embrace—"

APHRODITE: You have *got* to be kidding.

TIMAS:
  "Shower me with all your grace."
(APHRODITE *flings the remaining drops of nectar from the decanter in* TIMAS' *direction.)*

  "Aphrodite, I'm all on fire!
  Quench me! Quench me!—with your desire!"

(TIMAS *falls on the floor in a frenzied convulsion. Then she freezes, arms straight up in the air and eyes wide open, apparently in a state of rapture. APHRODITE walks around her, studying her.)*

APHRODITE: *(To the audience.)* If you were in my sandals, what would you do? *(A pause.)* Never mind. I have better things to do than entertain new arrivals on Lesbos. My arch-enemy is busy recruiting Sappho's students, and Hera is plotting to marry Sappho to that follower of hers—and to top it all off, Persuasion hasn't come back yet! Well... There's only one thing to do... *(She picks up the decanter.)* More nectar! (APHRODITE *exits. The voices of* ATTHIS *and* ANACTORIA *are heard from the wings.)*

ATTHIS: *(Offstage.)* Come on, Tory! We're almost there!

ANACTORIA: *(Offstage.)* Atthis, I *have* to get back and pack for the trip. Don't pull!

TIMAS: *(Coming out of her trance.)* Voices! Oh, goddess! My first Lesbians! *(She runs and hides behind the altar, as* ATTHIS *and* ANACTORIA *enter.* ATTHIS *is pushing* ANACTORIA.)

ANACTORIA: And don't push me, either! All right. We're here. This is Aphrodite's temple. Now, what is it you wanted to give me?

ATTHIS: You have to sit down.

ANACTORIA: Atthis, I don't have time for games—

ATTHIS: Please, Tory. Just sit. *(ANACTORIA considers for a moment, and then sits.)* Now… I want you to close your eyes.

ANACTORIA: Atthis—

ATTHIS: Please! Please! I promise, this won't take very long. Just close them. *(She does. ATTHIS looks at her for a moment, starts to touch her, backs off in fear, runs towards the altar and offers up a silent prayer. TIMAS, who has been peering out, ducks back out of sight. ANACTORIA opens her eyes.)*

ANACTORIA: What are you doing?

ATTHIS: *(Terrified.)* Nothing! *(Laughing lightheartedly.)* Nothing… Close your eyes… *(ANACTORIA looks at her with suspicion.)* This'll just take a minute… I promise. Close them. *(She does, and this time, ATTHIS moves next to her on the bench and puts an arm around her. She begins to kiss ANACTORIA's shoulder. TIMAS, is wide-eyed.)*

ANACTORIA: *(Opening her eyes.)* Atthis! What are you doing?

ATTHIS: *(Mortified.)* Um… You're supposed to keep your eyes closed. And not say anything.

ANACTORIA: Why?

ATTHIS: It's… It's a ritual! Yeah, a ritual.

ANACTORIA: Why am I always doing rituals with my eyes closed?

ATTHIS: Look, trust me. This is a ritual to Aphrodite, and it is a very good thing for women to do it before they get married.

ANACTORIA: Who told you that?

ATTHIS: Sappho.

ANACTORIA: Oh, well, Sappho would know.

ATTHIS: Yeah. So… ready?

ANACTORIA: Okay. *(She closes her eyes. ATTHIS resumes kissing her shoulder. She works up to the neck. ANACTORIA giggles.)*

ATTHIS: Keep your eyes closed.

ANACTORIA: This reminds me of when we were little girls together—remember? When we would sleep at each other's houses?

ATTHIS: Yes! That's what it's like.

ANACTORIA: And remember, I would put my face in your hair, and pretend I was a puppy. *(She snuggles in ATTHIS' hair. ATTHIS starts laughing.)*

ATTHIS: Wait, you're not letting me do the ritual. Close your eyes.

ANACTORIA: I don't want to. So what do you do next?

ATTHIS: *(Nervous.)* I… I'm supposed to take the tip of my tongue and follow it around the curve of your ear…

ANACTORIA: *(Screaming.)* No way!

ATTHIS: That's what I'm supposed to do.

ANACTORIA: It's going to tickle.

ATTHIS: Well, but then you get past that.

ANACTORIA: Past the tickling?

ATTHIS: Yeah.

ANACTORIA: To what?

ATTHIS: Well, you get this kind of warm… well, it's kind of a tingling… well, it's… Okay. You don't feel it in your ear at all.

ANACTORIA: Well, where *do* you feel it?

ATTHIS: *(At a complete loss.)* Look, do you want me to show you or not?

ANACTORIA: Okay. *(ATTHIS begins to kiss her ear, with ANACTORIA giggling. Then suddenly ANACTORIA closes her eyes and moans. ATTHIS pulls away in alarm.)*

ATTHIS: What?

ANACTORIA: *(Eyes still closed.)* No! Don't stop!

44

ATTHIS: You sure?

ANACTORIA: Yes. It's happening.

ATTHIS: *(Even more alarmed.) What's* happening?

ANACTORIA: The thing you feel not in your ear. Do it some more! *(ATTHIS kisses her ear again, and ANACTORIA moves her body against ATTHIS.)*

ATTHIS: Look, Tory, I'm getting scared. I… I have to tell you something.

ANACTORIA: *(Extremely aroused.)* What?

ATTHIS: *(Racing.)* Um… I went to Sappho, because I couldn't stand the thought of you leaving Lesbos and getting married, and she told me to kiss you, and then I said I didn't know how, and so she showed me, and that's what I'm doing, only now it doesn't seem like such a good idea.

ANACTORIA: Why?

ATTHIS: Because before, with Sappho, it was all—well, you know, not in the ear. But now, it's like all over my chest… like I can't breathe.

ANACTORIA: I know. Isn't it great?

ATTHIS: But… I'm scared.

ANACTORIA: I'm not.

ATTHIS: Yeah, but I am.

ANACTORIA: Then let me do it to you.

ATTHIS: You really want to?

ANACTORIA: What do you think? Come on. *(ANACTORIA kisses ATTHIS. ATTHIS disintegrates into her arms.)* So, what am I supposed to do next?

ATTHIS: I don't know. That's as far as Sappho showed me.

ANACTORIA: There has to be something else.

ATTHIS: Well, maybe there isn't.

ANACTORIA: No, there's something else. I *know* there's something else.

ATTHIS: I can ask her if you want me to.

ANACTORIA: Yes! And we can sleep together, like when we used to be girls—in honor of my leaving. And we can finish the ritual then.

ATTHIS: You really want me to?

ANACTORIA: Yeah! But I've got to go. I have to pack. I'll see you tonight.

ATTHIS: Yeah. *(ANACTORIA leaves, and ATTHIS slumps on the bench. TIMAS tiptoes furtively out from behind the altar.)*

TIMAS: Excuse me...

ATTHIS: Oh! You scared me!

TIMAS: Sorry...

ATTHIS: *(Grabbing her.)* Hey, have you been spying on me?

TIMAS: Me? No! I didn't see a thing. I just got here... Right off the boat, in fact. Timas. Timas from Crete. *(ATTHIS doesn't shake hands.)* Anyway, I just got here and I was wondering if you could direct me to Aphrodite's temple?

ATTHIS: Aphrodite's temple? This is it. You're standing in it.

TIMAS: I am? No kidding! Well, isn't that just the biggest coincidence in the world? Here I am looking all over for Aphrodite's temple, and all the time, I'm standing right in it! I'll be darned! Makes you wonder if all the things you've ever been looking for in your whole life might not be just standing right there, staring you in the face. *(Stepping in close to ATTHIS.)*

ATTHIS: *(Uncomfortable, stepping back.)* Yeah, well, look—I've got to go meet Sappho—

TIMAS: *(Circling to intercept her.)* Sappho! So you know Sappho... Quite a woman, isn't she? What about those poems of hers... are they something or what? "*Come goddess of Cyprus, and in golden cups serve nectar delicately mixed with delight...*" Is that a line or is that a line?

ATTHIS: Well, listen, I've got to run—

TIMAS: Oh, yeah, sure… and, uh… I've got to get busy with an offering to Aphrodite here, because if she doesn't help me, I don't know how I'll ever find Atthis.

ATTHIS: Yeah, well, good luck—*(She stops abruptly.)* Wait a minute… Did you say "Atthis?"

TIMAS: Yeah. Some student of Sappho's.

ATTHIS: What do you want with her?

TIMAS: Oh, I've got a message for her—from Sappho.

ATTHIS: What is it?

TIMAS: Sorry. It's confidential.

ATTHIS: But I'm Atthis.

TIMAS: No!

ATTHIS: Yes. Marathon runner. Winner of last year's Artemisian Games. That's me. Atthis.

TIMAS: Well, I'll be darned… Now *this* is too much! Absolutely too much. First I find the right temple by accident, and then I find the right person by accident… I can't believe it, can you? Seems to be some kind of fate, doesn't it?

ATTHIS: What's the message from Sappho?

TIMAS: The message?

ATTHIS: The message she wanted you to give me.

TIMAS: Oh, the message. Well, it had something to do with lessons.

ATTHIS: Lessons! Yes, what about the lessons?

TIMAS: She seemed to think you might be needing some more. Are these poetry lessons?

ATTHIS: Something like that. So what did she say?

TIMAS: Let me see... Oh, she said she wanted to give you another lesson, but she won't be able to do it until this evening. She wanted you to meet her here at sunset.

ATTHIS: At sunset?

TIMAS: That's right. Here at Aphrodite's temple. And she wanted you to be by yourself.

ATTHIS: Here, at sunset?

TIMAS: That's right. That's the message.

ATTHIS: Tell her I'll be here! Thanks, Timas. I owe you one. *(She exits.)*

TIMAS: Not after tonight, you won't! *(Turning exultantly to the altar.)* APHRODITE, QUEEN OF LOVE, HEAR MY PRAYER! *(APHRODITE stumbles on, carrying the now-full decanter.)*

APHRODITE: *(Shaking her ears.)* How could I not? Me and all of Lesbos.

TIMAS: Aphrodite, Goddess of Passion and Desire, thank you, thank you— oh, thank you...!

APHRODITE: What did I do this time?

TIMAS: You have granted the dearest wish of my heart...

APHRODITE: And that would be...?

TIMAS: ... to have the chance to practice the art of Sapphic love...

APHRODITE: Oh, Cronus! Is that all you girls can think about?

TIMAS: And thank you for inspiring me with the brilliant plan to disguise myself as Sappho in order to make love to Atthis, who is expecting me to teach her how to seduce Anactoria.

APHRODITE: *(To audience.)* Does any of this make sense to you?

TIMAS: And here's the beauty of the whole plan—Even though I've never made love to a woman in my life, Atthis will never know, because *neither has she*! *(TIMAS starts laughing hysterically.)*

APHRODITE: *(To audience.)* What the hell is she talking about?

TIMAS: O Aphrodite, I'll never forget you for this. In fact, as a special offering, I'm going to recite my poem for you again...

APHRODITE: Oh, no you don't. *(She snaps her fingers and TIMAS freezes.)* Sometimes I just love being a goddess. *(She turns TIMAS around to face the audience.)* She would make a nice fountain, don't you think? *(She pours herself a drink, talking to TIMAS.)* You haven't seen Persuasion, have you? Where is that girl? She can't really be amusing herself with the Goddess of Celibacy...? *(To TIMAS.)* That's too kinky, even for me! *(To audience.)* Well, never mind. The longer she stays away, the more anxious she'll be to come home. I'm planning a little surprise for her when she does. And I have a little surprise planned for Hera, too. *(To TIMAS.)* I like surprises, don't you? *(She pinches TIMAS's frozen cheeks.)*
Here... have a drink... *(She puts her goblet in TIMAS's hand and turns to go. Remembering she turns back and snaps her fingers. She exits as TIMAS unfreezes.)*

TIMAS: *(Starting in where she left off.)*

"The Queen of Love whose breasts are full . . . "

(She flings out her arms, and the contents of the goblet fly into the wings. Offstage, APHRODITE lets out a blood-curdling   screech. TIMAS notices the goblet.) Where did this come from? *(She shrugs, sets it on the altar, and resumes her recitation.)*

"The Queen of Love whose breasts are full . . . "
Whose hips are round, delect-a-ble, etc. "

(Lights fade on the recitation.)

BLACKOUT

END OF ACT

ACT II

SCENE 1

Lights come up on APHRODITE's temple on Lesbos. It's early evening of the same day. A YOUNG NAIAD, soaking wet, runs onto the set. She hides behind the altar. A troupe of NAIADS burst into the theatre, carrying gourds and bladders (bladders?) filled with water. The NAIADS should represent the classical Greek antecedent for a contemporary women's rugby team. [If the NAIADS are played by the same actors who were SAPPHO'S STUDENTS, they should wear fantastic make-up or masks in this scene.] The NAIADS, searching for their companion, race up and down the aisles, interacting with members of the audience. Suddenly, one of them spots the YOUNG NAIAD behind the altar. She lets out a whoop, and the NAIADS charge the stage. They chase the YOUNG NAIAD around the altar, giggling and screaming and throwing water. APHRODITE enters, carrying a decanter. Just then a NAIAD ducks, and APHRODITE receives a gourd of water in her face. The NAIADS freeze.

APHRODITE: *What* is going on here? What do you naiads think you are doing in my temple? Don't you know this is off-limits for your water-games? Look at the mess you've made! *(The NAIADS laugh.)* Get out of here! Go on! Get out of here—all of you! *(APHRODITE chases them off. She turns to the audience.)* Naiads! You have no idea what a problem they are. I've never met one yet, who knew the first thing about staying dry! *(Drying herself off.)* Not only have I lost my slave, but Hera is busy botching up my plans for Sappho—and, of course, Artemis, my arch-enemy, is on Lesbos right now trying to win converts to her particular brand of celibacy! The last thing I need is a gush of naiads saturating my sanctuary! *(She is mopping the altar as HERA enters.)*

HERA: Aphrodite—

APHRODITE: *(Not looking up.)* What is it now?

HERA: Could I speak with you for a moment?

APHRODITE: *(Realizing it's HERA, she shifts gears.)* Ah, Hera—just the goddess I wanted to see. Sit down, sit down... Make yourself comfortable... How are you?

HERA: Busy. I came here—

50

APHRODITE: And what perfect timing! I have just this minute tapped a new vintage of nectar, and I would consider it an honor if you would be the first to sample the crush.

HERA: No, thank you. Now what I came to talk about—

APHRODITE: But I insist! Here, just sample this bouquet... *(Pouring a cup.)*

HERA: *(More firm.)* No, thank you. What I wanted to say was—

APHRODITE: *(Sniffing.)* Delicate, but distinctive... a certain rambunctious quality that one would not expect to discover in a vintage with such an established reputation. Most remarkable... please... *(Holding the cup out to HERA.)*

HERA: No!

APHRODITE: But you insult my hospitality!

HERA: Aphrodite, I don't want your nectar. In fact, that's partly what I came to talk to you about. I find that since I gave up nectar, things have begun to look very different—

APHRODITE: *(Tasting.)* Ohhhhh! Really, Hera, you don't know what you're missing!

HERA: And neither do you. Take Sappho—

APHRODITE: Sappho?

HERA: Yes, the great poet of Lesbian love. Well, now that she is threatened with the loss of Gongyla, she is realizing just how unsatisfying all her little peccadillos have been.

APHRODITE: Unsatisfying?

HERA: Yes. And after centuries of attempting to create marriages out of the random couplings brought about by your lust, I realize that you have never been my ally. In fact, you and your slave are responsible for breaking up more marriages than you have fostered.

APHRODITE: Really, I don't believe I have ever sampled a nectar as... precocious as this— saucy, even! Hera— I *must* have your opinion—*(Holding out the cup.)*

51

HERA: Aphrodite, I said *no*.

APHRODITE: … as a *former* connoisseur. Just a taste. That's all I ask.

HERA: It is this obsession with nectar that keeps women from realizing their potential for joy.

APHRODITE: Joy! The very word! Joy— and yet I can detect a certain reserve, a reticence almost, in the aftertaste. But I can't be sure…

HERA: *(Her curiosity piqued.)* Do you mean it has a bite?

APHRODITE: No, it's too subtle for that… *(Another taste.)*… more like a kind of… wistfulness… Yes, that's it— just a hint of wistfulness— a trace of nostalgia, if you will— an essence which lingers on the palate to provide resonance without regret. I would say it is this quality of resonance which distinguishes the vintage and sets it apart from the banality of the ordinary crush.

HERA: I suppose it couldn't hurt just to *taste* it.

APHRODITE: No, no, you must stand for your principles. You were describing to me Sappho's sudden change of heart…

HERA: *(Reaching for Sappho's cup.)* I won't need a whole cup. I can just taste from yours.

APHRODITE: *(Snatching the cup away.)* I wouldn't hear of it. You were telling me about how an obsession with nectar robbed women of their potential for… what was it?

HERA: I can't recall. Perhaps a little taste will jog my memory.

APHRODITE: Joy! That's it! You said "joy."

HERA: *(Following APHRODITE.)* Did I? I don't remember.

APHRODITE: Yes, "joy." That would be a good name for the vintage, I think… "Joy." *(She sets down the cup, which HERA pounces on.)*

HERA: Here, let me see. *(Tasting.)* Mmm… interesting. *(Drinking deeply.)*

APHRODITE: But maybe "Delectation" would be better?

HERA: No, no, "Joy" is apt. *(Guzzling.)*

APHRODITE: But don't you feel it might be too strong a word—

HERA: *(Cutting her off.)* Not at all! The bouquet is subtle, but the nectar is full-bodied, and it does not disappoint.

APHRODITE: *(Refilling the cup.)* It's very gratifying to hear my experience confirmed by one who is in possession of so discriminating a palate.

HERA: You flatter me!

APHRODITE: Not at all. Your reputation is legendary.

HERA: *(Expanding fatuously under the influence.)* Well, I think you know I am not one to indulge in fatuous rhetoric regarding the virtues of a particular nectar, and so when I tell you it that this is the finest vintage of the millennium—as indeed it is— you can rest assured that I do so advisedly, and with the full weight of my authority as one whose conscientious and cultivated appreciation over the centuries as to the finer points of nectar culture has eminently qualified her in the sagacious appraisal of even the most rarified crush and that... *(A belch.)*... I know whereof I speak.

APHRODITE: *(Smiling.)* Who could doubt it? Another cup?

HERA: *(Holding out her cup.)* Oh, no... I won't hear of it...

APHRODITE: *(Steadying HERA's hand and pouring.)* But I insist.

HERA: *(Quite drunk.)* Oh, no, but *I* instist... insits... instit... *(She passes out. APHRODITE catches the cup as she goes down.)*

APHRODITE: Poor Hera. The Goddess of Marriage never could hold her nectar. Whatever will your followers do without your sober hand to guide them? *(She drags HERA offstage just as the voices of GONGYLA and SAPPHO are heard arguing. They enter. During their scene, the sun sets and the stars come out.)*

GONGYLA: No! And I don't appreciate being followed around and spied on!

SAPPHO: I'm not spying.

GONGYLA: Oh, Sappho— you don't expect me to believe that! You know I'm supposed to meet Gorgo here at Aphrodite's temple at sunset, to watch the meteor showers, and you have followed me here to make a scene.

SAPPHO: That's not true! I came out to watch the beautiful sunset and to compose a poem... Would you like to hear it?

GONGYLA: No—

SAPPHO: You look lovely in the moonlight, the way your hair—

GONGYLA: Stop it! Stop it! I'm not one of your eighteen-year old girls! You are not interested in marrying me, and you're just going to have to get over your jealousy about seeing me with someone else.

SAPPHO: Who said I wasn't interested in marrying you?

GONGYLA: You did, about a thousand times.

SAPPHO: What I meant was, I needed more time—

GONGYLA: It's been five years!

SAPPHO: I mean time to try it out. A trial period. A time when we're not seeing anybody else—

GONGYLA: Sappho, what do you think I've been doing for those five years? You were the one with all the girlfriends.

SAPPHO: How can I change, if you insist on holding the past against me? *(GONGYLA pulls away from her in exasperation.)* Listen, I'm willing to give it a try. *(GONGYLA gives her a look.)*

GONGYLA: Why is it every time I come close to leaving you, you find some trick to pull me back?

SAPPHO: Maybe because you're the only woman who has really loved me.
GONGYLA: Then why do you treat me so badly?

SAPPHO: *(Looking down.)* Maybe because you're the only woman who has really loved me.

GONGYLA: *(Crumbling.)* Oh, Sappho...

SAPPHO: Gongyla, give me this one chance. That's all I ask.

GONGYLA: I can't.

SAPPHO: Please. I won't see anyone but you for six months— I promise! We'll just date each other. And then, at the end of that time, if you still want to, I'll marry you. How about that?

GONGYLA: Do you really mean it?

SAPPHO: With all my heart. *(She puts her arm around GONGYLA and directs her attention to the moon, reciting:)*

> *"The stars around the fair moon fade*
> *Against the night,*
> *When gazing full she fills the glade*
> *And spreads the seas with silvery light."*

(She ends the poem with a kiss. During their embrace, GORGO enters with CLEIS.)

CLEIS: Mommy! Mommy!

GORGO: Looks like Mommy is busy, Cleis. *(GONGYLA pulls away from SAPPHO, embarrassed.)*

GONGYLA: We were just... Sappho was reciting a poem to me.

GORGO: I'm sure it was lovely.

GONGYLA: *(Flustered.)* Oh, it was.

GORGO: *(To SAPPHO.)* I envy your way with words.

SAPPHO: I have written a poem for you. Would you like to hear it?

GORGO: If that would please Gongyla.

GONGYLA: Oh, Sappho—

CLEIS: Mommy the stars are going to fall out of the sky tonight. Gorgo was telling me—

SAPPHO: It goes like this:

"... Yet I am not resentful in spirit,
...but have the heart of a small child."

CLEIS: Mommy, the stars are going to fall!

GORGO: It appears that mine already has. *(She turns to leave.)*

GONGYLA: No, wait! Sappho, will you excuse us?

SAPPHO: Certainly. Shall I see you tomorrow, then?

GONGYLA: *(Embarrassed.)* Yes.

SAPPHO: *(To GORGO.)* And here's another poem I call "Greetings to Gorgo:" *(Bowing.)*

"A very good day...
(Bowing again.)
To a daughter of very many kings...
(She bows again, starts to leave, and turns back for a final bow.)
A very good day!"
(She bows herself offstage.)

GORGO: Why didn't you want me to go?

GONGYLA: I felt I needed to explain—

GORGO: It's pretty self-explanatory.

GONGYLA: But I owe you an apology.

GORGO: *(Taking her hand.)* Gongyla, I knew you were still in love with Sappho, and I took my chances. You don't owe me an apology. I enjoyed every second I spent with you. I don't regret a minute. You are a wonderful person, and Sappho is a lucky woman to have you. I just hope you don't get hurt again.

GONGYLA: Oh, Gorgo, thank you. And you don't need to worry about me. Sappho and I have worked it all out. It's going to be different. *(GORGO smiles.)* I know what you think, but this time it really is. Sappho has promised to be faithful. You don't believe me, do you?

GORGO: It doesn't matter what I believe. It's *your* life and it's what *you* believe. I just hope it works out. You and Cleis deserve a good life. *(Kissing her gently on the cheek.)*

GONGYLA: Good-bye, Gorgo. Thank you. *(She turns to leave.)* Come on, Cleis.

CLEIS: But aren't we going to watch the stars?

GONGYLA: We'll watch them from our house, honey. Come on.

CLEIS: What about Gorgo?

GONGYLA: Gorgo's going to be staying here, honey. Now, come on.

CLEIS: Bye, Gorgo!

GORGO: Bye. *(CLEIS and GONGYLA exit, and GORGO turns to the altar, tears in her eyes. The sun sets during her speech and the stage becomes dim.)* Aphrodite, I should be angry with you, but I'm not. Who could be angry on a night like this—the stars so bright? What do they know about our little loves? And our lives—even a hundred years—are just a twinkle to them, or maybe a tiny streak of light, like a falling star. If I were Sappho, I would write a poem tonight. *(Voices are heard.)* What's this? Someone else must have come to see the meteor shower. *(She steps behind a pillar, and ATTHIS enters.)*

ATTHIS: Sappho? Sappho? Is that you? *(Turning to audience.)* I could have sworn I heard someone… *(She exits again, calling out:)* Sappho…! Sappho…!

GORGO: *(To audience.)* "Sappho!" Someone is meeting Sappho here tonight! *(ATTHIS re-enters and GORGO ducks back behind the pillar.)*

ATTHIS: I *know* I heard someone! Oh, what a night! What a glorious night! Just look at all those stars! And in a few short hours, I will know all the secret arts of love from the great teacher herself, Sappho!

GORGO: *(Peeking out from around the pillar, she speaks to the audience.)* Sappho! She couldn't even wait an hour!

ATTHIS: Aphrodite, I have never been a follower of yours, because I thought that love was just a waste of time, but now I know it is the real, true meaning of life, and tonight when I lie in the arms of my one true love, I will consecrate my life to your service, and to Sappho!

GORGO: Oh, this is too much! Poor Gongyla! I have to warn her. *(She exits.)*

ATTHIS: Tonight, when I spend the night with Anactoria, she will forget all about the wedding and the soldier, and we will stay on Lesbos and be Lesbians and students of Sappho forever! *(A cloaked figure enters.)*

TIMAS: Atthis! Psst! Atthis!

ATTHIS: Sappho! Is it you?

TIMAS: SHH! Keep your voice down.

ATTHIS: *(Rushing to her.)* Sappho? Why is your voice so deep?

TIMAS: *(Turning her face away.)* I've strained it with singing.

ATTHIS: Well, I was really glad when Timas gave me the message and all, because Anactoria and I kissed this afternoon, and it was wonderful, and she wants me to sleep with her tonight, and so I need you to show me the rest.

TIMAS: There's a lot to learn.

ATTHIS: Then we better get started, because she's waiting for me.

TIMAS: Yes. Well…

ATTHIS: We can skip the kiss. I've already learned that. Now what's next?

TIMAS: Well, it's not that simple… You have to… get in the mood.

ATTHIS: I *am* in the mood!

TIMAS: Yes, well, I'm not. *(Looking around.)* Here, look, someone's left some wine on the altar. Let's have a drink.

ATTHIS: I don't drink.

TIMAS: Well, you have to tonight. It's part of the sacred ritual.

ATTHIS: But I don't like the taste.

TIMAS: It doesn't matter. Here, drink. *(They both drink.)*

ATTHIS: Hey, this isn't wine! What is it?

TIMAS: I don't know, but it's great, isn't it?

ATTHIS: I'll say...! Let me have some more... *(Grabbing the decanter.)*

TIMAS: Me too! *(Grabbing it back.)*

ATTHIS: *(Grabbing it.)* To Sappho!

TIMAS: *(Grabbing it.)* To Sappho!

ATTHIS: That's you!

TIMAS: I know that. To Atthis!

ATTHIS: To Anactoria!

TIMAS: To Timas!

ATTHIS: Timas? Who's Timas?

TIMAS: The new student. The cute one.

ATTHIS: You mean the Cretan?

TIMAS: Right.

ATTHIS: To Timas! And Dika! And Hero! And Gyrinno! And Praxinoa!

TIMAS: To all the Lesbians on the island!

ATTHIS: To all the Lesbians all over the world! *(With that, ATTHIS finishes the last of the nectar, and tosses the decanter away.)* Oh, Gaia! I must be drunk! The stars are falling out of the sky!

TIMAS: No, I see them, too!

ATTHIS: We're both drunk!

TIMAS: It's like being drunk, only different.

ATTHIS: You want me to show you how I kissed Anactoria.

TIMAS: Sure.

ATTHIS: Well, first I kissed her like this. *(She demonstrates.)* And then like this. *(She demonstrates.)* And then like this. *(She demonstrates.)* And then *she* started kissing me.

TIMAS: You mean like this? *(She demonstrates.)*

ATTHIS: Yeah! And then we didn't know what else to do.

TIMAS: Did you try getting on the altar?

ATTHIS: No. Should we?

TIMAS: Of course. This is a ritual of love. Everybody does it on the altar.

ATTHIS: Really? Imagine that. On the altar.

TIMAS: Watch me. *(She falls off the altar three times.)*

ATTHIS: Here. I'll give you a hand. *(By now TIMAS is on the altar, and ATTHIS reaches up and pulls her off.)*

TIMAS: Thanks. Now, how are we going to get you up here.

ATTHIS: I'll just climb onto your shoulder. *(She gets on the altar and climbs onto TIMAS' shoulders facing her.)*

TIMAS: Hey! I can't breathe! Help! Help! *(The two of them reel around for a moment and then fall in a heap, with ATTHIS on top of TIMAS.)*

ATTHIS: Made it!

TIMAS: Yeah!

ATTHIS: So, where were we? *(APHRODITE appears at the side of the stage.)*

TIMAS: After the kiss…

ATTHIS: Oh, yeah, after the kiss… That's where I got stuck. *(APHRODITE crosses to TIMAS and whispers something in her ear, as ATTHIS struggles to stand up.)*

TIMAS: Wait a minute! *(She pulls ATTHIS back on top of her.)* I know what to do! *(Lights fade on the two lovers, as APHRODITE, laughing, exits into the shadows.)*

BLACKOUT

END OF SCENE

ACT II

SCENE 2

Lights come up on the Sacred Grove of ARTEMIS on Lesbos. It is the same evening, and the stars are as lovely as ever. PERSUASION stumbles onto the set, carrying her new bow. Completely out of breath, she collapses.

PERSUASION: I made it! I beat Artemis! Me, Persuasion—former slave! I just beat the Goddess of the Hunt to her own sacred grove! *(Lifting her head.)* Goddess— look at it! It's beautiful here! No altar, no columns— just the oak trees, and the wildflowers, and the little stream rippling over the rocks. *(She lies back.)* Oh, Gaia, I've never been so happy! I don't need anything or anybody! Just this little bow, and I can take care of myself anywhere! I'm free! I'm really free! *(Just then ARTEMIS enters. She is also winded.)*

ARTEMIS: There you are! How did you get here so fast?

PERSUASION: *(Pretending she is not out of breath.)* Fast? Was I fast? I don't know... I was too busy looking at the scenery...

ARTEMIS: Looking at the scenery! You ran like a jackrabbit!

PERSUASION: No, I didn't.

ARTEMIS: *(Lunging for her.)* You are a liar! You ran!

PERSUASION: *(Jumping out of the way.)* No, I didn't!

ARTEMIS: *(Grabbing her.)* Yes, you did! Admit it! You ran! You're still out of breath! *(PERSUASION screams, and the two women tumble over each other, laughing as they wrestle.)*

PERSUASION: No! No, I'm not!

ARTEMIS: Yes, you are!

PERSUASION: No, I'm not!

ARTEMIS: And you never leave your bow lying on the ground, because you never know who might come along and stomp on it—

PERSUASION: *(Shoving her out of the way.)* No, you don't! *(Grabbing one of ARTEMIS's arrows.)* I'll break your arrow... Truce?

ARTEMIS: *(Laughing.)* Truce. *(The women collect themselves. ARTEMIS splashes her face with water from the creek.)*

PERSUASION: *(Studying the arrow.)* So— how did I do for my first day?

ARTEMIS: You surprised me.

PERSUASION: Good or bad?

ARTEMIS: Good. No, better than good. I have never enjoyed another woman's company the way I enjoyed yours today.

PERSUASION: Really?

ARTEMIS: Really.

PERSUASION: Me, too. *(A silence.)* I have a confession to make. *(Another silence.)* When I begged you to take me as your student, I wasn't really interested in any of your subjects.

ARTEMIS: Then why did you want to be my student?

PERSUASION: Because I thought you were attractive, and I wanted to seduce you. *(Embarrassed, she laughs and covers her face.)* It's true, it's true! But now it seems ridiculous, doesn't it? *(ARTEMIS is stunned.)* Oh, but don't worry— I've gotten over it. It's like you said, girls only want to fall in love, because they're afraid to take care of themselves. And now, I don't feel like seducing anybody. *(She grabs her new bow and jumps up.)* I feel like shooting a bear!

ARTEMIS: You wanted to seduce me?

PERSUASION: *(Aiming at an imaginary bear.)* Don't take it personally.

ARTEMIS: I won't.

PERSUASION: See, it's hard to explain to someone like you who's always been independent. But it's a whole way of thinking, a whole different orientation.

ARTEMIS: I don't understand.

PERSUASION: Well, okay— I'll show you. Here— stand up. Okay, let's pretend you're me and I'm you and I'm teaching you how to shoot your bow. Okay. So you take your bow and draw it. And I'll be standing here showing you how to position your hands. *(She stands behind ARTEMIS to demonstrate.)* Now— if you're me— the old me— you're not listening to anything I'm telling you. You're just looking at my hand on top of yours, and all you're feeling is my breasts pressing against your back, and the only thing you're thinking about is how close my face is to yours, and what it would be like if you turned around, and put your arms around my waist and pulled my body close against yours, and then you pressed your lips against mine. *(She breaks away, laughing.)* And that's how I used to think before today.

ARTEMIS: *(Badly shaken.)* But you don't think like that anymore?

PERSUASION: Are you kidding? If I did, I'd be going crazy right now with the idea of us getting ready to spend the night out here together.

ARTEMIS: But you're not going crazy?

PERSUASION: Nope. I'm too busy thinking about all the things I'm going to learn tomorrow. Well— I think I'm just going to curl up by that old log over there. Good night, Andromeda. *(She starts to exit, has second thoughts, and crosses back to ARTEMIS, who is frozen in shock. PERSUASION steps close to her, gives her a light punch on the army, butch-buddy style, and exits.)*

ARTEMIS: Good night, Callisto… *(ARTEMIS sets her bow down. She begins to pace.)* What's the matter with me? My heart is pounding harder than it did when I raced Callisto up the mountain. And my knees! They're shaking like reeds in the wind. And all I can think about is the way her hand looked on top of mine—and the way her breasts felt, pressing against my back, and how it would feel if we… Oh, Gaia! It can't be! It isn't! Oh, Gaia! It is! *I'm in love!*

BLACKOUT

END OF SCENE

ACT II

SCENE 3

Lights come up on APHRODITE's temple on Lesbos. It is the next morning, dawn. Two figures are asleep on the altar. These are ATTHIS and TIMAS. TIMAS wakes up. Hung over, she falls off the altar.

TIMAS: Oh, Cronus! Where am I? *(Seeing the empty decanter.)* Oh! *(Seeing the cape.)* Oh! *(Seeing ATTHIS.)* Oh! I better get out of here, before she wakes up and realizes I'm not Sappho, and that it's morning, and that she didn't get to sleep with Anactoria on her last day, and boy, she's going to kill me! Good thing she doesn't know who I am! *(She exits quickly, leaving the cape behind. SAPPHO enters carrying a scroll.)*

SAPPHO: What a morning! Just look at that sky! What a glorious day! *(She sees ATTHIS, still asleep on the altar.)* What's this? Why, it's Atthis! What's she doing asleep on the altar? Oh— I forgot! Today is the day her girlfriend is leaving Lesbos to get married. Poor girl. She must have spent the night in prayer and fasting. No wonder she's so exhausted. *(Draping the cape over ATTHIS.)* Aphrodite, be kind to her. As kind to her as you have been to me! Gongyla is mine again! Thank you, gracious Cyprian! I composed this poem as an offering to you—*(She unrolls the scroll and reads it.)*

"You came; and it is well you came;
I was longing for you,
And now you have made my heart
Flame up and burn with love.
Bless you, I say,
Bless you three times—

(Suddenly GORGO enters, dragging GONGYLA.)

GORGO: There she is! There's your faithless fiancée— and caught in the act! Look at her! And celebrating her latest infidelity with a poem!

SAPPHO: Gorgo, what are you talking about?

GORGO: I'm talking about you and this… this… this… *(Indicating ATTHIS, who is still asleep.)… child*!

SAPPHO: What?

GORGO: I'm talking about how you lied to Gongyla, how you promised to be faithful, and then how you couldn't even wait an hour before rushing into the arms of another! How you didn't even have the decency to act out your betrayal behind closed doors, but how you had to humiliate Gongyla in front of all Lesbos, profaning the temple of Aphrodite with your lust and sacrificing your own pupil on the altar of your infantile desires.

SAPPHO: This is all very melodramatic, I'm sure, but I haven't the faintest idea of what you're talking about.

GORGO: *(Enraged.)* You had sex with this young woman, here— last night!

SAPPHO: Don't be ridiculous.

GORGO: It's too late to lie, Sappho! We've caught you in the act!

SAPPHO: Gorgo, this is too much. I've always known you were jealous of me, and because of that, I have tried to be tolerant of your slander—but this time you have gone too far. *(To GONGYLA.)* Gongyla, you can't believe what she's saying—

GONGYLA: *(Turning away.)* I don't know what to believe anymore.

SAPPHO: *(Surprised by GONGYLA's doubt, she turns angrily to GORGO.)* So you are accusing me of sleeping with Atthis last night—is that it?

GORGO: Yes.

SAPPHO: Then let's wake Atthis up and ask her.

GORGO: Go ahead.

SAPPHO: All right, I will. *(GONGYLA starts to leave.)* Wait, Gongyla, I want you to hear the truth. *(Angry, she shakes ATTHIS.)* Atthis, wake up! Wake up! *(ATTHIS, hung over, moans and rolls over. SAPPHO shakes her harder.)* Atthis, wake up! It's Tory's wedding day! *(ATTHIS sits up with a start. She shakes her head.)*

ATTHIS: Where am I?

SAPPHO: You're at Aphrodite's temple. You spent the night here.

ATTHIS: I did? *(Spying the empty decanter.)* Oh, I did... *(Holding up the cape.)* Sappho!

SAPPHO: I want you to tell Gongyla that you spent the night alone.

ATTHIS: *(Looking at GORGO and GONGYLA, and then turning back to SAPPHO.)* I spent the night with you.

GORGO: See! Even your students won't protect your lechery anymore! Gongyla, you heard her! You heard what her own student said!

SAPPHO: *(To ATTHIS.)* What do you mean, I spent the night with you?

ATTHIS: *(Getting angry.)* What do I mean? It was your idea to give me the kissing lessons—

GONGYLA: Kissing lessons?

SAPPHO: *(To GONGYLA.)* It's not what you think! We were just practicing.

GONGYLA: "Just practicing?"

SAPPHO: The kissing was… it was… academic.

GONGYLA: "Academic?"

GORGO: Come on, Gongyla, we've heard enough.

SAPPHO: *(Grabbing ATTHIS.)* Tell them the truth, you little monkey-face!

ATTHIS: The truth! You tricked me into getting drunk and then I passed out—

SAPPHO: *(Shaking her.)* Liar! You liar!

ATTHIS:… and instead of spending the night with Tory, I spent it out here with you—

SAPPHO: *(Still holding ATTHIS.)* Liar! She's lying!

ATTHIS: … and you made love to me! *(ATTHIS breaks free and pushes SAPPHO away. SAPPHO loses her balance and falls backwards on the ground. ATTHIS runs off.)*

SAPPHO: Gongyla—Believe me! I—

GONGYLA: *(Covering her face, she crosses to exit.)* No more, Sappho—no more! I just can't take any more!

GORGO: *(Turning back to SAPPHO as she escorts GONGYLA off.)* You have finally gone too far. I always knew you would. And now I am going to see that your school is closed, and your poems banned, and that you yourself are exiled from Lesbos! *(She exits with GONGYLA. SAPPHO is too shocked even to stand up. Just then ARTEMIS enters. She is still disguised as Andromeda.)*

ARTEMIS: Excuse me, but aren't you Sappho?

SAPPHO: *(Turning towards her, dazed.)* Am I?

ARTEMIS: The great poet of Lesbos...?

SAPPHO: Whatever.

ARTEMIS: *(Dropping fervently to one knee.)* Teach me, O Sappho—! Teach me the art of love! *(SAPPHO does a take.)*

BLACKOUT

END OF SCENE

ACT II

SCENE 4

A spotlight at the front of the stage. APHRODITE appears in the spotlight, rubbing her hands.

APHRODITE: *(To audience.)* Well, that's it! It's over. You can all go home now. I won. *(Breaking into a victory dance.)* I won! I won! I won! *(To audience.)* It was beautiful, wasn't it? I couldn't have staged it better myself... Artemis, the great Goddess of Celibacy, down on her knees to Sappho—*my* Sappho!—groveling for lessons in love! So much for her little school of self-reliance! So much for her self-righteous celibacy! So much for her and Hera's little conspiracy to overthrow the Goddess of Love! And now that Sappho is all mine, Lesbos shall be all mine, and every woman everywhere shall be mine, mine, mine— ! *(Suddenly HERA staggers on. She is badly hungover.)*

HERA: Not so fast, Aphrodite!

APHRODITE: Why, Hera, I didn't expect to see you up before noon... tomorrow.

HERA: *(Speaking thickly.)* You haven't won and it's not over yet, because *I* am still in the race!

APHRODITE: *(Mockingly.)* Would you care for a drink?

HERA: No! Your nectar may be intoxicating, but it can never satisfy the craving for love.

APHRODITE: *(Proposing a toast.)* A noble sentiment—and nobly expressed.

HERA: *(Cutting her off.)* I know you don't have any respect for me, and I haven't given you much reason to, but I'm not giving up on what I believe in.

APHRODITE: And what is that?

HERA: Commitment. Oh, I know you think it's a joke—

APHRODITE: Hera! How can you say that? I think all your followers should be committed.

HERA: I may not be as clever as you are, Aphrodite, but there is one weapon I possess, and I think I have underestimated its power.

APHRODITE: Oh?

HERA: Yes. Sincerity. And I sincerely care about these women.

APHRODITE: What women?

HERA: These women! *(Indicating the audience.)* These women right here. They deserve something better than one-night stands, broken promises, and endless heartaches. And they deserve something better from the Goddess of Marriage than some shambling, conservative, people-pleasing, passive-aggressive nectar-holic! These women deserve to be loved! *(Turning suddenly on APHRODITE.)* Aphrodite, this is war!

BLACKOUT

END OF SCENE

ACT II

SCENE 5

HERA's temple. The altar is festooned with flowers for Anactoria's farewell party. It's still morning. SAPPHO'S STUDENTS are singing in two groups as they hold hands and dance around the altar. ANACTORIA and TIMAS are among the dancers. TIMAS is struggling to follow the steps of the dance.

STUDENTS I:

"The moon rose full: the women stood
As though within a sacred wood
Around an altar..."

STUDENTS II:

"And thus at times, in Crete, the women there
Circle in dance around the altar fair;
In measured movement, treading as they pass
With tender feet the soft bloom of the grass."

STUDENTS I	STUDENTS II
(This is sung as a round.)	

"Come to me, O ye graces,	
Delicate, tender, fair;	
Come from your heavenly places,	*"Come to me, O ye graces,*
Muses with golden hair.	*Delicate, tender, fair;*
Come to me, O ye graces,	*Come from your heavenly places*
Delicate, tender, fair;	*Muses with golden hair.*
Come from your heavenly places,	*Come to me, O ye graces,*
Muses with golden hair."	*Delicate, tender, fair;*
	Come from your heavenly place
	Muses with golden hair

(Suddenly ATTHIS bursts in. TIMAS steps quickly behind a pillar.)

ATTHIS: Tory! *(Deep in the dance, ANACTORIA ignores her.)*

STUDENTS I	STUDENTS II
"Come to me, O ye graces,	
Delicate, tender, fair;	

Come from your heavenly places,	*"Come to me, O ye graces,*
Muses with golden hair.	*Delicate, tender, fair;*
Come to me, O ye graces,	*Come from your heavenly places—*

ATTHIS: *TORY! (SAPPHO'S STUDENTS stop singing.)*

ANACTORIA: What is it, Atthis?

ATTHIS: I have to speak to you— privately.

ANACTORIA: *(To the STUDENTS.)* Go on and practice the dance. I'll be there in a minute. *(She steps downstage with ATTHIS. The STUDENTS continue the dance. TIMAS remains behind her pillar.)*

ATTHIS: *(Urgent.)* Tory, I'm really sorry about last night. Sappho got me drunk, and I passed out—

ANACTORIA: *(Distracted.)* It's fine—don't worry about it. Listen, my parents will be here any minute, and we have to practice the dances for the wedding cycle—

ATTHIS: Tory, there's no one I love as much as I love you, and I wanted to sleep with you. I've never wanted anything so much in my life—

ANACTORIA: It's *okay.* Look, I need to get back in the circle now. Do you want to be in the dance?

ATTHIS: *(Grabbing her.)* Listen, Tory, I'm never going to see you again if you go through with this! I love you, and I know you love me—*(Her voice has become very loud. The STUDENTS stop dancing to look at ATTHIS. ANACTORIA is embarrassed.)*

ANACTORIA: *(Quietly.)* Let go of me, Atthis. You're embarrassing me.

ATTHIS: *(Louder and not letting go.)* No! Not until you listen to what I have to say: I love you, and I know you love me more than some stupid soldier your parents want you to marry—

ANACTORIA: *(Struggling to get away.)* Stop it!

ATTHIS: *(Escalating.)* No! Listen to me! And yesterday, at Aphrodite's temple, when I kissed you, you liked it—

ANACTORIA: *(Frantic that the STUDENTS will hear.)* No, I didn't!

ATTHIS: *(Continuing to escalate.)* Yes, you did—and you kissed me back, and you wanted to do more than just kiss, only I didn't know how—and you asked me to come sleep with you—

ANACTORIA: I did not!

ATTHIS: *(Shouting.)* Tory, I love you! I love you! *I* want to marry you! *(She tries to kiss ANACTORIA. ANACTORIA slaps her hard and pulls away.)*

ANACTORIA: How could you do this to me on my wedding day? I never want to see you again! *(She runs off. SAPPHO'S STUDENTS run after her. ATTHIS starts to follow her, but checks herself. Turning in her rage, she shoves the flowers off the altar and exits in the opposite direction. TIMAS peers out from behind the pillar. After a moment she goes after ATTHIS.)*

BLACKOUT

END OF SCENE

ACT II

SCENE 6

Lights come up on the Sacred Grove of ARTEMIS. It's morning of the same day. ARTEMIS enters carrying a scroll. She is attempting to memorize a poem.

ARTEMIS: *(Reciting.)*

   "You came; and it is well you came..."
(Starting over.)
   "You came; and it is well you came..."
(Forgetting the line again.)
   "You came; and..."
(Reading the line from the scroll.)
   "You came; and it is well you came..."
(Closing her eyes, she recites rapidly.)
   "You came; and it is well you came..."
   "You came; and it is well you came..."
   "You came; and it is well you came..."
(Taking a deep breath, she starts over:)
   "You came; and it is well you came..."
(Just then PERSUASION enters, carrying her bow and a string of trout.)

PERSUASION: Yo!

ARTEMIS: *(Turning in surprise.)* Callisto!

PERSUASION: *(Smiling and holding up the fish.)* I came and it is well I came.

ARTEMIS: I... I was... just memorizing some poetry.

PERSUASION: You're kidding? Look at the trout I caught. They were in the trap we built this morning! Look at them all—

ARTEMIS: Callisto, I need for you to listen to this poem.

PERSUASION: Right now?

ARTEMIS: Right now.

PERSUASION: Why?

ARTEMIS: I just need for you to.

PERSUASION: Can I clean the fish while you read it?

ARTEMIS: I think it would be better if you didn't.

PERSUASION: All right.

ARTEMIS: *(She sits. ARTEMIS begins to pace. Suddenly she drops to one knee and begins a stiff recitation:)*

"You came; and it is well you came;
    I was longing for you,
    And now you have made my heart..."
(This is as far as she has memorized. She reads the rest of the poem from the scroll.)
    Flame up and burn with love.
    Bless you, I say,
    Bless you three times—
    Bless you for just so long
    As you and I have been parted!"

(She rolls up the scroll and stares expectantly at PERSUASION, who is at a loss as to how to respond.)

PERSUASION: That's it? *(ARTEMIS, unable to speak, nods fervently.)* Well, it's very nice. *(ARTEMIS is still staring at her.)* Did you write it yourself? *(ARTEMIS shakes her head.)* Who wrote it?

ARTEMIS: Sappho.

PERSUASION: Oh. That's nice. *(ARTEMIS hasn't moved.)* She gave it to you?

ARTEMIS: I bought it.

PERSUASION: You bought it?

ARTEMIS: I traded her my school.

PERSUASION: *(Horrified.)* You traded your school for that poem? *(ARTEMIS nods.)* Why?

ARTEMIS: *(Mechanically, miserably.)* Because I don't care about my school. All I care about is you.

PERSUASION: *(Looking around.)* Is this a joke?

ARTEMIS: No.

PERSUASION: *(At a complete loss, she holds out the string of trout.)* Here— why don't you clean some fish? Maybe you'll feel better. *(ARTEMIS stands rigidly immobile. PERSUASION steps back in agitation.)* I don't know what to say. This wasn't supposed to have happened. It's going to ruin everything!

ARTEMIS: How?

PERSUASION: How? Because now we can't be friends anymore.

ARTEMIS: Why not?

PERSUASION: Because lovers aren't supposed to like each other!

ARTEMIS: They're not?

PERSUASION: No! Lovers are... lovers are... *(Throwing the trout at ARTEMIS.)*... they're nothing but *slaves!* (She exits, stumbling into HERA on her way out. ARTEMIS starts after her, but HERA catches her arm.)*

HERA: Artemis, wait! I have to talk to you!

ARTEMIS: Not now! I have to find Callisto!

HERA: "Callisto?" You mean "Persuasion?"

ARTEMIS: *(Stopping dead.)* Persuasion?

HERA: That girl who just ran by? That's Persuasion.

ARTEMIS: You mean, Aphrodite's slave?

HERA: You didn't recognize her?

ARTEMIS: No. *(Hitting herself on the head.)* Of course! The Slave of Love! Oh, goddess— no wonder she ran away! Poor girl...

HERA: Artemis, I need your help.

ARTEMIS: *(Turning suddenly towards her.)* And I need yours. But we haven't got much time! Come on! *(She drags HERA out.)*

BLACKOUT

END OF SCENE

ACT II

SCENE 7

Lights come up on the Sacred Grove of ARTEMIS. It's afternoon of the same day. ATTHIS enters. She is out of breath, and covered with scratches and bruises. She has been crying.

ATTHIS: Artemis! Hear me! It is I, Atthis of Lesbos, the most worthless of your followers! *(Kneeling.)* I have betrayed you, Artemis. I have betrayed you and everything you stand for. I sold out my celibacy for a night of drunken debauchery. I abandoned my true love in her hour of need, and I have brought dishonor to your sacred name. I have come here to offer up my worthless life, that the wolves may eat my flesh and the birds may pick my bones, and the green forgiving grass may grow over whatever remains of Atthis of Lesbos, false follower of Artemis! *(She takes a dagger from her tunic and points it towards her breast. Just then GONGYLA enters.)*

GONGYLA: Atthis, no!

ATTHIS: Gongyla, I betrayed you, too.

GONGYLA: Put the knife down. *(ATTHIS doesn't move. GONGYLA sighs.)* Please, Atthis… it's making me terribly nervous. *(ATTHIS drops her arm.)*

ATTHIS: I'm sorry.

GONGYLA: You don't need to apologize. In fact, I should thank you.

ATTHIS: For what?

GONGYLA: For making me face the truth about Sappho.

ATTHIS: But I was the one who asked her for lessons in the art of love. It wasn't her fault.

GONGYLA: *(Taking the knife.)* Oh, Atthis, you are such a little warrior. I love your fine spirit, and so will some lucky girl, someday.

ATTHIS: There could never be another love for me after Tory.

GONGYLA: *(Smiling.)* You are so young.

ATTHIS: *(Bristling.)* But my love is true.

GONGYLA: What about Tory's?

ATTHIS: If I had been able to make love to her, things would have been different.

GONGYLA: Would they?

ATTHIS: She wouldn't be marrying that soldier.

GONGYLA: Are you sure?

ATTHIS: She loves me! I know she loves me! And she would have known it too, if we'd been lovers.

GONGYLA: It takes more than love to make a relationship.

ATTHIS: Like what?

GONGYLA: People have to want the same things. And Tory wants to have babies, and a husband who supports her, and she wants to live near her parents and do things that make them happy. And because that's the life she wants, it doesn't matter how much she loves you.

ATTHIS: I can't believe Tory would want anything so boring and stupid.

GONGYLA: And I can't believe that Sappho wants to go on having affairs with women half her age—but, you know something? Just because I can't believe something, doesn't mean it isn't true—and isn't going to hurt me.

ATTHIS: So you think, even if I'd slept with her, Tory would still have gotten married?

GONGYLA: Probably—but just because Anactoria has her life, doesn't mean you can't have yours. And someday you will meet a girl who loves you as fiercely and as tenderly as you love her.

ATTHIS: *(Concerned.)* What about you?

GONGYLA: Me? *(Smiling.)* I think I need to be by myself for a while. *(Just then SAPPHO enters, out of breath.)*

SAPPHO: Gongyla! I have to speak to you! *(ATTHIS jumps up, ready to confront her. Just then GORGO enters.)*

GORGO: Gongyla—I've been looking for you—

SAPPHO: *(Grabbing GORGO.)* What do you want, you troublemaker? *(Just then, TIMAS enters, out of breath.)*

TIMAS: Wait! Wait! Everybody wait! I have something to say! Listen! I have something to say! *(Everyone is silent and TIMAS is startled by their silence. She becomes embarrassed.)* I… uh… I… uh… okay, okay… it was me. *(A long silence.)* I was the one Gorgo saw at Aphrodite's temple. I was wearing a cape, and I pretended I was Sappho, so Atthis would kiss me, and I didn't really think it was going to get so serious, but there was this stuff on the altar, and we both thought it was wine—

ATTHIS: You! You mean it wasn't Sappho?

TIMAS: It was me.

SAPPHO: *(To GONGYLA.)* You see! I told you! It was one of Gorgo's tricks.

GORGO: I had nothing to do with it.

TIMAS: No, she didn't have anything to do with it. I thought it up all by myself when I saw Atthis kissing her girlfriend, and I just wanted to be a Lesbian, too, and I didn't think it would end up like this. *(To ATTHIS.)* Honest. *(To GONGYLA.)* And I didn't know Sappho had a girlfriend—

GONGYLA: It's all right, Timas.

TIMAS: *(To ATTHIS.)* So—can we be friends… do you think? *(ATTHIS turns away from her outstretched hand. TIMAS turns to SAPPHO.)* I guess you don't want me at your school anymore, either?

SAPPHO: *(Smiling.)* I guess I do.

TIMAS: Really? You mean I can stay? *(To ATTHIS.)* Atthis, I'm really sorry.

GONGYLA: Timas, I think you should go join the other students for their dancing.

TIMAS: *(Still trying to connect with ATTHIS.)* I didn't know you and Tory were—

GONGYLA: Timas—now.

TIMAS: Yeah… sure… *(A last look at ATTHIS before she exits.)*

GONGYLA: *(Putting her arm around ATTHIS.)* I could use some help with Cleis this afternoon. Why don't you take a day off from school.

ATTHIS: *(Appreciating her kindness.)* Thanks… thanks. *(To SAPPHO.)* I'm sorry…

SAPPHO: Skip it. *(To GONGYLA.)* Gongyla, I need to speak to you.

GONGYLA: There's nothing left to say.

SAPPHO: But I'm innocent! You heard her!

GONGYLA: Sappho—and I want to tell you, too, Gorgo—I am not ready to be with anyone. I have a lot of things to sort out, and a little girl who needs my attention.

GORGO: When you're ready, will you let me know?

GONGYLA: You'll be the first. *(SAPPHO starts to protest, but GONGYLA cuts her off.)* Good-bye, Sappho.

SAPPHO: Wait! *(GONGYLA kisses her and exits with ATTHIS.)*

GORGO: *(To SAPPHO.)* I owe you an apology.

SAPPHO: Gorgo, you don't "owe" me anything. You don't have anything that's mine, and you never will. *(GORGO is left standing on the stage.)*

BLACKOUT

END OF SCENE

ACT II

SCENE 8

Lights come up on APHRODITE's temple. It's afternoon of the same day. PERSUASION is kneeling before APHRODITE. She is chained to a pillar, and her wrists are manacled. Her head is bowed, and we cannot see her face. APHRODITE paces during her speech, stopping periodically to prod the silent PERSUASION.

APHRODITE: So you see, ungrateful girl, I was right. The world is not a kind place to an ugly woman with no talent, is it? Without the taste of my nectar, it was unbearable, wasn't it? Well, you're not the first young woman to make that little discovery, and you won't be the last. Don't flatter yourself on your uniqueness. You girls are all the same. And you always come back to me, don't you—? expecting me to greet you with open arms, with tears in my eyes—to press you to my bosom and welcome you home with a thousand tender endearments—isn't that what you expected...? Slave! Yes, a foolish, but persistent fantasy on the part of young women. But you found out that the Goddess of Love was not so inclined to overlook your insubordination, was she? No, you found your mistress was not so eager to take you back as you expected, was she? You see, Persuasion, once a woman has defied me, it becomes necessary to resort to somewhat more coercive measures to reinforce the bonds of our "mutual commitment." *(Laughing, she crosses downstage.)* It is unfortunate that you chose this particular time for your little insurrection, as both my challengers are on the brink of capitulation. Indeed, one—Artemis, in fact—has already surrendered. Yes, Artemis, your great heroine. You didn't know that, did you? Yes, the Goddess of the Hunt has become one of my converts. No doubt seduced by some little chippy of Sappho's. You see, Persuasion, no one is immune to my charms. How foolish you were to think you could succeed where even the Goddess of Celibacy would fail... But, as I was saying, your timing is most unfortunate, for I shall shortly have need of the services of a faithful messenger, when I am named Supreme High Goddess of all Lesbos—and by extension, the whole world! *(Suddenly there is a loud crash off stage.)*
What? Who's there? *(She exits left. HERA and ARTEMIS enter right. HERA is carrying a formidable labrys.)*

HERA: There she is!

ARTEMIS: Callisto! *(PERSUASION lifts her head and then turns away.)*

HERA: Here—take the labrys and strike the chains from her. I'll keep a lookout, in case Aphrodite comes back. *(ARTEMIS crosses to PERSUASION, who shrinks away from her.)*

ARTEMIS: Callisto, hold out your arms and let me cut your chains!

PERSUASION: My name is Persuasion. Leave me alone. I don't want to be free.

ARTEMIS: Your name is Callisto, and you are the woman I love, and I know you ran back to Aphrodite, because I scared you—but I can't believe you really want to be her slave.

PERSUASION: Well, I do.

ARTEMIS: But why?

PERSUASION: Because it's clean.

ARTEMIS: I don't understand.

PERSUASION: I'm her slave; she's my mistress. I do what she tells me, and she provides for my needs. We don't have to pretend to like each other. I know what's expected of me, and I know what to expect. It's honest. It's clean.

ARTEMIS: Meaning that my love for you isn't?

PERSUASION: Exactly.

ARTEMIS: How do you know? You never even gave me a chance.

PERSUASION: Because it's always the same. It always ends in slavery.

ARTEMIS: But it doesn't have to.

PERSUASION: But it always does.

ARTEMIS: You were in love with me when I wasn't interested in you.

PERSUASION: Yes.

ARTEMIS: I'm still the same Artemis.

PERSUASION: No, you're not! You're in love!

ARTEMIS: Look... You loved me for my independence, didn't you?

PERSUASION: Yes.

ARTEMIS: But don't you see, it's easy to be independent when you don't love anybody but yourself! Just like it's easy to fall in love, when you don't know how to be independent. Freedom and love have to go together or they don't mean anything at all. *(A long silence.)* You're right, Callisto—

PERSUASION: "Persuasion."

ARTEMIS: Persuasion. You're right... I can't rescue you. You have to do that for yourself. *(She drops the labrys next to PERSUASION.)* And I hope you do.

APHRODITE: *(Calling from offstage.)* Persuasion...!

ARTEMIS: I love you. *(PERSUASION looks away.)*

APHRODITE: *(Offstage.)* Persuasion! Why don't you answer me!

ARTEMIS: Good-bye, Callisto.

PERSUASION: *(Bitterly.)* "Persuasion!"

APHRODITE: *(Offstage.)* Persuasion!

ARTEMIS: *(Crossing quickly to HERA.)* Come on, let's get out of here. *(They exit.)*

APHRODITE: *(Still offstage.)* So you don't think you need to answer me, is that it? I guess your chains aren't persuasive enough, are they? It seems I'll have to resort to a little more direct mode of discipline... *(APHRODITE appears upstage or at the back of the theatre with a whip. She practices with it as she approaches PERSUASION. Meanwhile, PERSUASION, experiencing a change of heart, has lunged for the labrys and is frantically chopping away at her chains, her back turned to APHRODITE.)*

APHRODITE: ... Not that I haven't encountered this kind of stubbornness before . . . But I must say, I had not expected it from a slave on whom I have showered so many favors. Indeed, no whip could ever cut so deeply or sting so brutally as the ingratitude to which I am perpetually subjected by women

84

such as yourself, women from whom I have every right to expect satisfaction. Scalded by scorn, branded by contempt, and tortured on the rack of cold indifference—such are the torments of the Goddess of Love—Persuasion, do you hear me? Persuasion! *(PERSUASION finally breaks through the chains.)*

PERSUASION: *(Calling.)* Artemis! Artemis! I'm free! I love you! Come back! I love you! *(ARTEMIS and HERA re-enter.)*

APHRODITE: What is going on here?

PERSUASION: Aphrodite, I'm not your slave anymore. I have liberated myself, and I am in love with Artemis, and she is in love with me, and there's nothing you can do about it, because it's not your kind of love. *(To HERA.)* And it's not yours either.

HERA: I don't know what "my kind of love" is anymore, now that I'm sober. But I'm very happy for you.

APHRODITE: Well, it isn't going to matter in the least, because as long as Sappho is *my* priestess, neither *you*... *(Indicating ARTEMIS.)* ... nor *you*... *(Indicating HERA.)*... are going to have anything to say about love. *(Just then SAPPHO enters.)*

PERSUASION: It's Sappho!

APHRODITE: Yes, and she's come to worship *me*. Too bad she can't see how foolish you all look. *(SAPPHO crosses in front of the goddesses and tosses a scroll onto the altar.)*

SAPPHO: Well, there it is—my last poem! Aphrodite, I'm through with you!

APHRODITE: What?

HERA: *(To APHRODITE.)* Be quiet!

SAPPHO: I hope you're satisfied. I will never write another line. You have betrayed me, Aphrodite. You have betrayed me after all my years of faithful service to you. In fact, you were the only one to whom I *was* faithful. Ironic, isn't it? And in the end you're the one who has betrayed me the most. *(She unrolls the scroll and reads:)*

> *"The moon hath left the sky;*
> *Lost is the Pleaids' light;*
> *It is midnight*

And time slips by;
But on my couch, alone I lie."

(She tosses the poem back on the altar and turns to leave just as TIMAS enters.)

TIMAS: Wait, Sappho! It's me, Timas.

SAPPHO: Timas?

TIMAS: The new student. The one who made all the trouble…

SAPPHO: What do you want?

TIMAS: I just wanted to thank you for letting me stay at your school—

SAPPHO: *(Turning to go.)* Go to bed.

TIMAS: *(Chasing after her.)* Sappho?

SAPPHO: What?

TIMAS: There's something else I wanted to tell you… *(SAPPHO waits.)* If it hadn't been for your poems when I was growing up, I wouldn't have known what was going on… you know, with me and other girls. I might have thought there was something wrong with me. But because of your poems, I knew I just needed to be a Lesbian. You saved my life. *(SAPPHO still says nothing.)* Well… I just wanted you to know that.

SAPPHO: *(Studying the young woman.)* Timas, no one is even going to remember us.

TIMAS: You don't really believe that.

SAPPHO: Don't I?

TIMAS: No. It's in your poem.

SAPPHO: It is?

TIMAS: *(Reciting.)*
"Somebody,
I tell you,
Will remember us hereafter…"

86

SAPPHO: I wrote that?

TIMAS: Yes, and it's true. They will remember. I mean, people make fun of me because I'm different, but sometimes I can see things, and tonight I can look out at the stars and see the faces of generations and generations of new Lesbians—and not just Lesbians on Lesbos, but Lesbians all over the world—in countries we don't even know about—! and they are listening to your words, Sappho! They are listening, and they are loving. *(SAPPHO smiles and puts her arms across TIMAS's shoulders.)*

SAPPHO: And do you write poetry?

TIMAS: *(Blushing.)* Me? Oh, no… Well, a little…

SAPPHO: Can you recite any of your poems?

TIMAS: You really want me to?

SAPPHO: Come on… let's walk back. *(They start to exit, walking slowly. SAPPHO's arm is still around TIMAS, butch-buddy style.)*

TIMAS: Well, there is this one called "Ode to Aphrodite."

SAPPHO: Good title.

TIMAS: *(Reciting.)*

 "Aphrodite, whose breasts are full, etc."

(They exit as TIMAS recites. APHRODITE turns triumphantly to ARTEMIS and HERA.)

APHRODITE: You see? She's still mine! Sappho is still mine!

ARTEMIS: And you can keep her, Aphrodite. You deserve each other.

APHRODITE:And what about you, Hera? Do you concede my claim to Sappho?

HERA: As long as the arts of Persuasion are wedded to the ideal of independence, the women of Lesbos shall have nothing to fear from you, or your nectar, or your priestesses.

APHRODITE: Time will tell, my dear Hera, time will tell.

HERA: And in the meantime, will you join us in celebrating the union of Persuasion—

PERSUASION: Callisto.

HERA: ... Callisto and Artemis?

APHRODITE: Why not? And will you join me in a toast?

HERA: When your nectar is a sacrament and not a sacrilege.

APHRODITE: *(Lifting her cup sarcastically)* To a former slave and her fallen goddess! *(Just then there is a wild war whoop from offstage.)*

PERSUASION: Here come the naiads! *(The NAIADS burst in, sopping wet, as usual. They chase each other around the altar. APHRODITE tries to drive them off with her whip.)*

APHRODITE: Stop that! Stop it! Get out of here! You're getting everything wet, you wicked girls! Get out of here! Go on! Get out! *(Suddenly the NAIADS turn on APHRODITE. They seize her whip and lift her onto their shoulders. She lets out a bloody scream.)*

APHRODITE: Ahhhh! Stop it! What are you doing? Put me down! Put me down this instant! Do you hear me? Persuasion, do something! Hera! Help! Stop it! Hera! Artemis! Help me! Help me! You are ruining my outfit! *(The NAIADS run off with APHRODITE, as the goddesses laugh.)*

PERSUASION: *(To HERA.)* Do you think we should rescue her? *(There is a piercing scream followed by a loud splash.)*

HERA: What? And ruin my outfit?

ARTEMIS: Hera, will you bless our union?

HERA: I would be honored. *(She lifts APHRODITE's cup.)* To Callisto and Artemis, and... *(Turning to the audience.)* ... to all of us former slaves and fallen goddesses—Blessed be! *(She throws the contents of the glass out over the audience, and the lovers embrace.)*

BLACKOUT

END OF PLAY

[It would be appropriate for APHRODITE to take the last curtain call sopping wet.]

About the playwright...

Carolyn Gage is a lesbian-feminist playwright, performer, director, and activist. The author of seven books on lesbian theatre and sixty-three plays, musicals, and one-woman shows, she specializes in non-traditional roles for women, especially those reclaiming famous lesbians whose stories have been distorted or erased from history. Her collection of plays *The Second Coming of Joan of Arc and Selected Plays* won the Lambda Literary Award in Drama, the top LGBT book award in the US.

Her play *Ugly Ducklings* was nominated by the American Theatre Critics Association for the prestigious ATCA/ Steinberg New Play Award, an award with given annually for the best new play produced outside New York. It won the Lesbian Theatre Award from *Curve Magazine*, and a documentary on the play premiered at the Frameline International Film Festival in San Francisco. *The Anastasia Trials in the Court of Women* was named national finalist for the Jane Chambers Award given by the Association for Theatre in Higher Education. Her one-act, *Harriet Tubman Visits a Therapist*, was presented at Actors Theatre of Louisville in the Juneteenth Festival of African American plays. It was a national winner of the Samuel French Off-Off Broadway Festival, and is included in Random House's anthology *Under 30: Plays for a New Generation.*

Gage's musical, *The Amazon All Stars* is the first lesbian, full-book musical ever published by a mainstream play publisher. Published by Applause Books, it is the title work of an anthology of lesbian plays that was a national finalist for the Lambda Literary Award. Her manual on lesbian theatre production, *Take Stage! How to Direct and Produce a Lesbian Play* was published by Scarecrow Press.

Gage has lectured at Tisch School of the Arts at New York University, and she has been a Guest Lecturer at Bates College in Maine. She has won numerous state and national awards, including the Lynda Hart Memorial Grant from the Astraea Foundation. She spent three months as a Artist-in-Residence at the Wurlitzer Foundation in Taos, New Mexico.

One of the most prolific feminist playwrights in the world, Carolyn Gage is a dynamic speaker and a powerful role model.

Sappho in Love

www.ingramcontent.com/pod-product-compliance
Lightning Source LLC
Chambersburg PA
CBHW030402290526
45785CB00004B/1874